CAPTAIN FANTASTIC
STEVEN GERRARD

MATT AND TOM OLDFIELD

DINO

Published by Dino Books
an imprint of John Blake Publishing Ltd
3 Bramber Court, 2 Bramber Road,
London W14 9PB, England

www.johnblakepublishing.co.uk

www.facebook.com/johnblakebooks 🅵
twitter.com/jblakebooks 🅣

First published in paperback in 2017

ISBN: 978 1 78 606 219 2

British Library Cataloguing-in-Publication Data:

A catalogue record for this book is available from the British Library.

Design by www.envydesign.co.uk
Cover illustration by Dan Leydon
Background image: Shutterstock

Printed in Great Britain by CPI Group (UK) Ltd

1 3 5 7 9 10 8 6 4 2

Papers used by John Blake Publishing are natural, recyclable products made
from wood grown in sustainable forests. The manufacturing processes
conform to the environmental regulations of the country of origin.

Every attempt has been made to contact the relevant copyright-holders, but some
were unobtainable. We would be grateful if the appropriate people could contact us.

For Noah and the future Oldfields to come

Looking forward to reading this book together

TABLE OF CONTENTS

ACKNOWLEDGEMENTS

First of all, I'd like to thank John Blake Publishing –
and particularly my editor James Hodgkinson – for
giving me the opportunity to work on these books
and for supporting me throughout. Writing stories for
the next generation of football fans is both an honour
and a pleasure.

I wouldn't be doing this if it wasn't for Tom. I owe
him so much and I'm very grateful for his belief in
me as an author. I feel like Robin setting out on a
solo career after a great partnership with Batman. I
hope I do him (Tom, not Batman) justice with these
new books.

Next up, I want to thank my friends for keeping

me sane during long hours in front of the laptop. Pang, Will, Mills, Doug, John, Charlie – the laughs and the cups of coffee are always appreciated.

I've already thanked my brother but I'm also very grateful to the rest of my family, especially Melissa, Noah and of course Mum and Dad. To my parents, I owe my biggest passions: football and books. They're a real inspiration for everything I do.

Finally, I couldn't have done this without Iona's encouragement and understanding during long, work-filled weekends. Much love to you.

CHAPTER 1

ANFIELD FAREWELL

It was a sunny afternoon as the two teams walked out at Anfield, Liverpool in red and Crystal Palace in yellow. On the pitch, the players lined up opposite each other to form a tunnel. Liverpool only had ten – there was one very important player still to come.

'Ladies and gentlemen,' the announcer began. 'This club has been privileged to have many fantastic footballers putting on the red shirt over the years but this player, this man, is truly unique. Please raise your cards now to welcome your captain on to the pitch for his final game at Anfield, the one and only STEVIE GERRARD!'

Everyone in the stadium clapped and cheered as

Stevie walked on with his three daughters, Lilly-Ella, Lexie and Lourdes. As he moved down the line, the Crystal Palace players gave him high-fives. They had so much respect for all that Stevie had achieved.

Around the centre circle, Stevie waved to all of the fans who had helped to make his Liverpool career so special. He would never forget them, just as they would never forget him. In front of him, at the Kop end, was the most amazing thing he'd ever seen. There were lots of flags showing his name and face, and the fans were holding up cards that spelt out 'SG' in huge letters with the number '8' in the middle. Along the side of the pitch, the cards spelt out 'CAPTAIN'. The fans sang his chants again and again.

Steve Gerrard, Gerrard
He'll pass the ball forty yards
He shoots the ball really hard
Steve Gerrard, Gerrard

Stevie Gerrard is our captain
Stevie Gerrard is a red

CAPTAIN FANTASTIC

Stevie Gerrard plays for Liverpool
A Scouser born and bred

Stevie had to fight back tears as he got ready for kick-off. The club meant so much to him but after seventeen seasons, it was time to leave Liverpool. He had touched the iconic 'This is Anfield' sign outside the dressing room for the last time as a Liverpool player and captain.

The Liverpool supporters sang 'You'll Never Walk Alone' at the top of their voices. Stevie would always get goosebumps when he heard the club anthem. The team was desperate to get a final win for Stevie and when Adam Lallana scored the opening goal, he ran to give Stevie a big hug. 'That was for you!' he said.

But Crystal Palace weren't interested in giving Stevie a happy ending to his Liverpool story. They scored two goals and suddenly Liverpool were risking defeat.

'I can be the hero one last time,' Stevie said to himself. 'I really want to score!'

He felt tired after another long season and every shot he took went wide of the goal. The fans called for him to keep shooting, but in the last minute Palace made it 3–1.

It was disappointing to end a club career with a defeat but it wasn't really about the result. It was about a captain saying goodbye to his supporters, and the supporters saying goodbye to their captain.

The Liverpool players came back out on to the pitch wearing '8 GERRARD' T-shirts.

'A whole team of Gerrards would be amazing!' Martin Škrtel joked with his teammates. 'We would definitely win the Premier League!'

As Stevie walked out, the singing started all over again. He waved to his wife, Alex, and his parents, Paul Sr and Julie, in the crowd. Without their love and strength, he couldn't have become such a superstar. The club presented him with a trophy in the shape of the Number '8' and then it was time for Stevie to speak. He had been dreading this moment for weeks. It was one thing scoring goals in front of 44,000 people but speaking was very different. He was very nervous but with Lourdes in his arms, he took the microphone.

'I am going to miss this so much,' he said, looking up into the stands. 'I'm devastated that I'll never play in front of these supporters again.'

Stevie thanked everyone at Liverpool: all of the coaches and managers he had played under, and all of the teammates that he had played with. He was so grateful to everyone for all of their support over the years.

'I've played in front of a lot of supporters around the world but you're the best,' he concluded. 'Thank you very much.'

It didn't feel real – was he really leaving Liverpool? When he was young, Stevie never thought that he would leave his beloved club. Top teams had tried to sign him but he had stayed loyal. It wasn't about money; it was about love and pride. Now he was off to play in the USA, for a new club in a new league – but nothing would ever compare to Liverpool.

He had played 709 games, 503 in the Premier League, and he had scored 119 goals. With his team, he had won the Champions League, the UEFA Cup, the FA Cup twice and the League Cup three times. He had so many amazing memories from his time at Anfield. It was here that he had grown up from a fierce-tackling skinny kid to become a world-class, goalscoring midfielder and the captain of club and country.

It had been an amazing journey for this young Liverpool fan from Huyton, and Stevie had loved every minute of it.

CHAPTER 2

HUYTON

'Paul! Stevie! Dinner!' Julie shouted from the front door of their house on Ironside Road. They lived in a nice community where everyone knew each other and the kids were free to play in the streets without any danger. The offer of food was usually enough to bring the children back home.

After waiting a minute, Julie heard the sound of running feet and saw her two sons turn the corner at the top of the road. Stevie was sprinting as fast as he could, with his little arms and legs moving very quickly. Behind him, Paul Jr was sprinting too. He was three years older than his brother and so it wasn't a very fair race.

Julie was so pleased that her sons were best friends. Of course, they had arguments sometimes but mostly, they couldn't be separated. Stevie wanted to do everything that his older brother did and Paul Jr wanted to look after his younger brother. The Gerrards were a very close, happy family. They didn't have lots of money, but there was always food in the cupboards and they always ate together.

Just as Stevie got near to their house, Paul Jr caught him.

'Got you!' he shouted as he grabbed his brother's shirt. Stevie slowed to a stop, panting hard. One day when he was a bit older and stronger, he would be able to outrun Paul Jr. But for now, he was just really hungry.

'What's for dinner, Mum?' he asked. Looking down at his trousers, he worried that he might be in trouble.

'Nothing until you two have a wash,' Julie replied. 'Paul, didn't I tell you to keep Stevie away from the mud? Look at you both – you're filthy!'

After a quick change of clothes, the family sat

down for a feast of burgers and chips. Paul Jr and Stevie wolfed the food down and asked for more. Their dad, Paul Sr, couldn't help but smile.

'I remember when I was a growing lad like you two. I could eat anything I wanted and I was still as thin as a rake. Now, look at me!' he said, patting his belly. His sons laughed and laughed.

'Stevie, take Granddad Sidney his tea and sit with him for a bit please,' Julie said once their meal was over. Her father was very ill and she looked after him in their house.

Stevie loved spending time with Granddad Sidney. He was a very kind man who loved his grandsons. Sidney had lots of great stories about Liverpool Football Club and his adventures with the British Navy. Stevie sat in a chair next to his bed and listened to him for hours.

'How's the football going?' Sidney asked.

'Paul's teaching me how to kick the ball really hard,' Stevie replied excitedly.

'Good, because I want a Liverpool player in this family,' Sidney said. He wasn't well enough to leave his bedroom but he watched lots of sport on TV. He often gave Julie money to buy his grandsons the latest Liverpool kit.

'Dad, you're spoiling them!' she told him, but it made him happy.

Stevie's other granddad, Granddad Tony, lived just down the street at 35 Ironside Road. Stevie loved having all of his family nearby. Some of his cousins and neighbours supported local rivals Everton instead of Liverpool and that made the derby matches really exciting. In the summer, all of the local families sat out in the street, eating and drinking and having a great time. The Bluebell Estate in Huyton was a great place to grow up.

After chatting to Granddad Sidney for a while, Stevie went looking for Paul Jr. His older brother had a bigger bedroom with a bigger bed and a bigger wardrobe. Stevie only had a tiny room but he didn't mind because Paul Jr was his hero.

The two spent a lot of time playing together, but sometimes, Paul Jr needed his own space. When he was hanging out with his friends, he didn't always want his younger brother around. One day, when he was sitting on a wall talking to a group of older boys, he pushed Stevie away, saying, 'Go home and find some mates!'

Any fights between Stevie and Paul Jr only ever lasted a few hours. Then they were best friends again. Every weekend, they sat on the sofa with their dad to watch *Match of the Day* on TV. When the theme music started, they all sang along. It was their favourite part of the week.

'That could have been me, kids,' their father said as they cheered a Peter Beardsley goal for Liverpool. Paul Sr had been a good footballer when he was young but he hurt his knee when he was fifteen. Now, he worked as a builder in the city, but he still encouraged his sons to excel at sport. 'And now, that can be you two!'

Julie didn't always watch the games but she was a Liverpool fan too – she didn't have any choice in such a football-mad family. If the boys weren't watching videos of old Liverpool victories, they were at Anfield watching Liverpool play live. Stevie loved standing on the Kop with his dad and brother. The atmosphere was amazing and the singing never stopped. It was extraordinary to watch players like Kenny Dalglish and John Barnes running down the Liverpool wing. The pitch looked so big and green, and Stevie was desperate to play there one day.

'Right, bedtime!' Julie would say when *Match of the Day* was over. Paul Jr and Stevie groaned but it was late and they could barely keep their eyes open. Slowly, they made their way upstairs.

'Paul, can we do more shooting tomorrow?' Stevie asked as he brushed his teeth. He would dream about the Beardsley goal for at least the next week.

'Sure – you'll be scoring great goals in no time!' his brother replied.

CHAPTER 3

HAPPY STREET

'Please let me come and play!' Stevie said to his brother as he rushed out of the front door with a football under his arm. Stevie was counting down the days until he could play his first match at 'Happy Street', the football pitch at the end of their road.

'How many times do I have to tell you? You're still too young,' Paul Jr told him. 'Some of the boys are really big and you'll get hurt.'

Stevie was six and his brother was nine but some of Paul Jr's friends were even older. They didn't want to play with a small, skinny kid who might cry if he fell over on the concrete. But Stevie wasn't scared;

he would do anything to make his debut at Happy Street.

'Please! I'll even go in goal if you want,' Stevie said. He wasn't giving up and his brother knew it.

'Fine, you can play but just don't embarrass me.'

'Yes!' Stevie shouted, jumping into the air. He was already in his lucky Liverpool shirt. He had been waiting for this moment for years. As they walked along the row of identical houses, Stevie thought about what he could do to impress the others. He needed to make sure that they let him play every day.

There were eight boys waiting for them by the goal and there were no cars in sight.

'Perfect – five-a-side,' Paul Jr said, taking a shot.

'Wait, Stevie isn't playing, is he?' their cousin Jon-Paul asked. 'He's tiny!'

'Yes he is but only for today and he says he'll play in goal,' Paul Jr replied. 'Don't worry about hurting him – he's my brother!'

He quickly picked the teams so that no-one else could complain, and made sure Stevie was on his team. Stevie stood between the goalposts and waited to make a save. The ball came flying towards him at great speed and he caught it bravely.

'Nice save, Stevie!' one of the boys shouted and Stevie's smile got even bigger.

Stevie was only wearing shorts but he was fearless. To stop goals, he dived to his right and he dived to his left. He had blood running down his knees but his team was winning thanks to a goal from Paul Jr. Suddenly, one of Stevie's teammates, Sammy, twisted his ankle.

'Are you alright?' Paul asked as Sammy sat on the floor in pain.

'No, I can't keep playing,' Sammy replied, trying to wiggle his ankle.

There was only one solution. 'Okay, do you think you could stand in goal?' Paul asked Sammy, helping him him back on his feet. Sammy nodded and limped towards the goal.

'Stevie, you're playing out on pitch now!' Paul shouted.

This was his big opportunity. Stevie rushed forward, he ran and ran and he made some good tackles but his teammates weren't passing to him. He was in lots of space on the right and his brother was dribbling towards goal.

'Paul! Pass to me!' Stevie shouted. At first, Paul Jr ignored him but then he saw that Stevie was the only free option. When he passed to him, he expected his little brother to lose the ball or take a weak shot. But Stevie controlled the ball and calmly looked up to see who he could pass to. Mark had made a run and Stevie played a perfect ball through the defence to him. Mark took one touch and scored.

Paul Jr jumped on Mark to celebrate but Mark ran over to Stevie. He gave him a big hug. 'What a pass, little man!' he shouted and Stevie felt on top of the world.

When he next got the ball, Stevie tried to dribble past one of the biggest boys but the boy pushed him to the floor. It really hurt his bleeding knees but Stevie was determined not to cry. He just had to get used to the hard tackles.

'Are you okay, Stevie?' Paul Jr asked, but his brother was already back on his feet and running into space. Paul Jr smiled; there was no stopping Stevie now that he was playing at Happy Street.

Jon-Paul scored two quick goals and suddenly it was 2–2. It was nearly dinner time and there were no streetlights at Happy Street when it got dark. Everyone was getting tired, except Stevie.

'Right, next goal wins!' Paul Jr shouted.

Stevie was desperate to be the hero. He chased the ball all around the pitch, trying to win tackles. He was like a bee buzzing around his opponents. They tried to swat him away but he wasn't giving up.

Paul Jr won the ball in defence and looked up. His teammates on the left and right were being marked closely. Stevie was their furthest player forward and suddenly he dashed into space. Paul Jr passed the ball and his little brother was through on goal. They had practised shooting in the back garden for hours and hours. Paul Jr hoped that Stevie would know what to do.

Stevie could hear a defender running towards him and he could see the goalkeeper in front of him. The goal looked so small – it seemed impossible to score.

If he waited too long, the defender would catch up with him, or the goalkeeper would run out and block him. It was time to shoot. Stevie aimed for the bottom corner and pulled back his leg. He struck the ball with as much power as his little legs could manage.

The ball rocketed towards the goal. The keeper dived but he couldn't quite reach it.

Goooooooooooooooaaaaaaaaaaaaaaaaaaaaaaaaaaa aaaalllllllllllllllllllllllllllllllll!!!!!

Stevie couldn't believe it. Paul Jr and Mark lifted him up into the air – he was the match-winner!

'What a finish, mate!' Sammy shouted as he hobbled from the goal to join in the celebrations.

This was the best day of his life so far. Stevie couldn't wait to tell the story to his dad. Paul Jr let him proudly carry the match ball back to their house.

'Stevie's going to be a great player when he's older,' Jon-Paul said.

Paul Jr nodded. 'Our family will have at least one professional footballer!'

CHAPTER 4

MIDFIELD TERRIER

'John Barnes gets the ball on the left-wing, he dribbles past one defender and then another and then another! He's in the penalty area and he's just got the goalkeeper to beat... what a goal!' Stevie shouted as he kicked the ball into the net and then jumped into the air. He imagined that he was John Barnes playing for Liverpool and that his teammates like Ian Rush and Peter Beardsley were running over to congratulate him.

While he waited for the other boys to arrive for games at Happy Street, Stevie loved pretending to be his hero. Barnes was the most exciting player in the country, a really skilful midfielder who played for Liverpool and England. Stevie loved all of the Liverpool players but Barnes was the one he always wanted to be.

Stevie worked hard to improve his dribbling skills and his shooting but he wasn't a winger like Barnes. He was a midfield terrier who never stopped running from one great tackle to the next. If Stevie was around, no-one on the Bluebell Estate got more than a few seconds on the ball – and it was the same on the St Michael's school playground too.

Classes really got in the way of football, but break time and lunch time were awesome. Stevie took a packed lunch with him so that he could play for longer. He would take a few bites of a sandwich and then start kicking the ball. During lessons, he would write out the teams in the back of his exercise book so that everyone was ready to go.

'Right, you guys can kick off,' Stevie shouted.

The games were massive, hour-long battles. On a Sunday night, Julie laid out Stevie's clean school uniform but by Monday afternoon, it was already dirty. His smart shoes only ever lasted a few months.

'Sorry Mum!' he said when he got home from school. Julie was furious but eventually she had to relent – you couldn't stop Stevie from playing football. Even on a cold winter's evening nothing could stop the boys from playing on the estate, and Stevie would shiver in his shorts and Liverpool shirt.

One day, a car parked on Happy Street. A relative was visiting one of their neighbours and, of course, they weren't to know this concrete space was the 'pitch' where the boys played football. Stevie went straight up and knocked on his neighbour's front door.

'Hi, Stevie,' Mrs Fowler said as she opened the door. 'How can I help you?'

'Hi, Mrs F. Do you know anything about that car?' he asked, pointing towards the concrete space.

'Yes, that's my sister's car – she's on a day trip from Wales.'

'That's nice – could she move it, please?' Stevie asked.

'Oh,' Mrs Fowler replied. She was very surprised by Stevie's assertive request but he was smiling very politely. 'I don't know where else she can park...'

'I'm sorry, Mrs F, but that's our pitch!' Stevie interrupted.

Fifteen minutes later, the car was gone and the boys' game could finally begin.

Sometimes Stevie joined in games with his school friends but as fun as it was, the level was too easy for Stevie and so he preferred to challenge himself against his brother and his older friends. From Monday to Friday he played with them on the estate. At weekends, though, he was desperate to join them in their local Under-10s team, Tolgate. So one day, he went down to a training session there.

'Hello, can I join in please?' he asked the coach who was setting out the cones.

The coach looked at the small, skinny boy in front of him. 'How old are you, kid?' he asked.

Stevie thought about lying but he knew that his brother would tell the truth. 'Seven, but I play with older boys all the time, I promise.'

The coach shook his head. 'I'm sorry, lad, but you're just too young. Come back in a couple of years.'

On the walk home, tears streamed down Stevie's face. He kicked stones and coke cans as hard as he could. It wasn't fair; just because he wasn't the same age as the other boys didn't mean that he wasn't good enough. They should have given him a chance.

'I'll show them!' he said to no-one.

Stevie worked even harder on his touch and his toughness. He couldn't do much about his size or strength but being brave and fearless made a big difference. In one game on Happy Street, a twelve-year-old used his shoulder to push Stevie into the fence. His face scratched against a nail and he could taste the blood. But still Stevie didn't complain. He just ran across the road to Granddad Tony's house.

'Granddad, this won't stop bleeding,' he said and in ten minutes he was back out on the pitch with a big plaster on his face.

Paul was a good player but he didn't have the same determination as his younger brother. All Stevie wanted to do was become a top professional footballer like John Barnes, and finally, when he was eight, he took his first step towards Liverpool

Football Club: he joined a Sunday League team called Whiston Juniors.

'Great tackle, Stevie!' the manager, Ben McIntyre, shouted from the touchline.

It was only a training session but that didn't matter to this kid. He only ever played at 110 per cent and he had it all: not only pace and bravery but also skill and power.

'Okay, calm it down,' Ben told him. He needed to protect his star player from injury.

Stevie was the best player of his age that Ben had ever seen. The big question was how good could he become?

CHAPTER 5

SCOUTED
BY LIVERPOOL

As a Liverpool youth coach and scout, Dave Shannon often got calls about exciting new football talent in the local area. He didn't have much spare time and so it was always difficult to work out which players were really worth watching. One night, Dave was relaxing at home when the phone rang. It was Ben McIntyre.

Straightaway Dave knew that this wasn't one of those normal phone conversations. Ben McIntyre was a good friend and the manager of Whiston Juniors. If he was calling about a young player then Dave trusted his advice.

'I've got this great kid that I think you should

really come and watch,' Ben said. 'We've got a game on Sunday if you're free?'

Dave could hear the excitement in Ben's voice. This youngster must be really good. 'If he's that good, just bring him to our training on Wednesday.'

'Sure, I'll do that,' Ben agreed.

'What's his name?' Dave asked, grabbing his notebook and a pen.

'Steven Gerrard.'

At the training session, at Vernon Sangster Sports Centre, Dave Shannon watched from the sidelines with his fellow coaches Hughie McAuley and Steve Heighway. The Under-9s practice was about to begin, and Stevie had arrived. He wasn't as big and strong as some of their other players but often kids grew a lot at a later age. This boy was quiet but Dave could see the focus in his eyes. He wasn't there to mess around – he was there to show what he could do.

In the sprinting tests, Stevie was one of the quickest and in the passing exercises, he showed that he had good technique. Dave was impressed but he was waiting to see him in the five-a-side match at the end

– that was the real test. It took Stevie a few minutes to get involved but soon he was running the show. He won the ball back and ran forward. He looked up, played a good pass and then moved into space.

Dave looked at Hughie and nodded – he didn't need to say anything.

Stevie was everywhere: rushing back to defend and then rushing forward to shoot. This was only his first session but he was already a leader, showing his teammates where he wanted them to be for the pass. His self-belief and ambition were clear for all to see. These were the very important qualities that the coaches looked for in their young players.

'Wow, that kid's a natural,' Steve said when the practice was over. 'I don't think he played one bad pass.'

'And what a tackler!' Hughie added with a big smile on his face. 'Did anyone ever get past him?'

Dave shook his head. 'He's special, that's for sure. Let's get him back next week.'

*   *   *

'Well played today!' Stevie said to his teammates Michael Owen and Jason Koumas after another win for the Liverpool youth team. Michael was a brilliant striker who scored lots and lots of goals. Stevie had never seen anyone who was so good at finishing. Jason was a skilful midfielder who loved doing tricks and setting up lots of goals. Together, the three of them had a great understanding of each other's abilities on the pitch.

'You too, mate,' Michael replied as they walked to the changing room. 'Do you ever get tired? I get tired just watching you racing around the pitch!'

It was a dream come true for Stevie to be playing for Liverpool, the club he loved. There was a nice, friendly atmosphere there, and Dave, Hughie and Steve were great coaches. With their support and guidance, he was rapidly improving as a central midfielder. When he watched the first team play on the Kop, Stevie thought about the path ahead. The top was a long way off, but he was well on his way.

At Whiston Juniors, Stevie's performances had attracted lots of attention from Premier League scouts. He had a rare combination of skills: passing, shooting, dribbling *and* tackling. Ben wanted to keep his superstar but he also knew that Stevie was destined for bigger things. Manchester United, West Ham and Everton were all interested but when Dave asked him to train with Liverpool, Stevie's mind was made up.

'There's no better place to play than Anfield!' Paul Sr told Stevie. To have a son playing for Liverpool was a thrill for him too. Paul Sr and Julie made sure that Stevie always looked smart and behaved himself, as respect was very important at a club like Liverpool.

From his first training session with the Under-9s, Stevie knew that this was where he wanted to be. He was working hard and competing with other really good young players. Like him, they loved winning and absolutely hated losing. Even when Stevie was exhausted, he never stopped.

'So what shirts are we wearing on Wednesday?' Jason asked.

For the five-a-side matches at the end of training,

the boys were put into teams based on the colour of their shirts. The skills and possession exercises were brilliant too but the half-an-hour match was what everyone looked forward to. Stevie, Michael and Jason made sure that they wore the same kit, so that they were always on the same team. No-one could beat them when they played together. Stevie won the ball and passed to Jason. Jason dribbled past defenders and passed to Michael. Michael always scored.

'Let's wear the grey Liverpool away shirt,' Michael said and they all agreed.

CHAPTER 6

HILLSBOROUGH

Eight-year-old Stevie sat in the living room with his parents and his brother. No-one said a word as they watched the tragic images from the Hillsborough stadium in Sheffield. Liverpool were about to play in the semi-finals of the FA Cup against Nottingham Forest. It was supposed to be an exciting day for the club but something terrible had happened.

Too many fans had been let into the stadium at the last minute and there was an awful crush. Stevie was so shocked by what he saw on the screen. The BBC reported that many people had died. Ninety-six. No-one could believe it.

'How did this happen?' Julie said to no-one in

particular. There were tears in her eyes. 'I hope we don't know anyone that went to the game today.'

Stevie found it very difficult to sleep that night. He couldn't stop thinking about the disaster. The horrible images kept running through his head.

The next morning, there was a knock at the door. People didn't usually come to see them so early on a Sunday. Stevie ran downstairs and opened it. It was Granddad Tony and he looked very upset as he walked into the living room. He didn't say anything until the rest of the family had sat down. As he waited, Stevie was very worried.

'I'm sorry, I've got some really bad news,' Tony began. His voice was shaking with emotion. 'Jon-Paul was one of the ninety-six at Hillsborough.'

Stevie didn't even know that his cousin had gone to the game. He went to Anfield all the time but his mum had bought him a ticket for the semi-final as a special treat. Jon-Paul lived on a different estate in Liverpool but he often came to play at Happy Street with Paul Jr and Stevie. They all loved football and

Liverpool Football Club in particular. They were more like brothers than cousins.

Again, there was silence at 10 Ironside Road, as they tried to take in the terrible news. There was a lot of crying and a great deal of anger and confusion. The Hillsborough disaster was a heartbreaking day for Liverpool: for the city, the football club and the Gerrard family. Stevie would never forget the 15th April, 1989, or his wonderful cousin Jon-Paul.

Jon-Paul was only ten years old, the youngest victim of the tragedy. He wasn't much older than Stevie when he travelled to Sheffield. On a different day, Stevie could have been with him at Hillsborough. He felt so lucky to be alive.

'Are you okay, love?' Julie asked him, squeezing his hand. This was such a difficult thing for a young child to understand. Stevie nodded but he couldn't speak.

When he went back to training a week later, Stevie was more determined than ever to succeed. The football club was still mourning the loss of ninety-six fans but the players had to carry on and show lots of strength. Stevie had an amazing opportunity to do something that would make Jon-Paul and the rest of the family so proud.

He would become a Liverpool hero and he would do it for Jon-Paul.

CHAPTER 7

A VERY LUCKY BOY

Playing for Liverpool never stopped Stevie from playing on Happy Street. If he was at home and he wasn't too tired, he would walk out of his front door and see if there was a game going on. There was almost always someone there with a ball.

'Stevie!' the others cheered whenever he turned up. The local kids were very proud of their friend who showed all the potential of becoming a top Liverpool player, but they never went easy on him. They tackled hard and they took the matches very seriously. This was their Anfield and they wanted to show Stevie that he wasn't the only talented player on the Bluebell Estate.

'Do you think you're too good for us now that you're a star?' they teased him.

'I've always been too good for you!' Stevie teased back.

One day, he was having a kick-about with Mark and the ball rolled into a nettle bush along the side of the pitch.

'I'll get stung if I put my arm in there,' Stevie said. He was wearing a short-sleeved shirt and so he pulled his socks up as high as possible and tried to get the ball with his foot instead.

The nettles were too thick and Stevie couldn't see the ball. He was getting annoyed because he wanted to keep playing. He kicked as hard as he could and his right foot hit something.

Owwwwwwwwwwwwwwwwwwwwwwwwwwwwwwwwww!!!

Stevie fell to the ground in agony. He had never felt pain like this. 'Mark, help me! I can't get my leg out of the bush!'

Mark took a look and nearly fell to the ground too. 'Stevie, you've got to stay really still, okay? I'm going to get help.'

Finally, Stevie managed to look down; a big, rusty garden fork was stuck in his big toe. It was even worse than he had expected. A neighbour came down and tried to pull it out but he couldn't. Stevie screamed and cried. This was really bad. What if he could never play football again?

'Don't worry son, we're here!' his dad shouted as he ran over. Stevie could see the worry in Paul Sr's face.

An ambulance arrived and took Stevie to the hospital. It was the worst journey of his life. Every bump in the road was so painful.

'Slow down!' he screamed each time.

The doctor was very worried. 'The toe may well be infected and so we're going to have to take it off,' he told Paul Sr and Julie, but Stevie heard the scary news too.

Paul Sr wasn't happy about that idea and so he called Steve Heighway, the Liverpool youth coach.

'Stevie's had an accident and they're talking about amputating his toe!'

Steve drove straight to the hospital with the Liverpool physio Mark Waller and they tried to change the doctor's mind. 'The kid's football career will be over if you do that. Please try everything else first.'

The surgeon agreed to remove the fork and then look at the damage. There was a big hole there, but Stevie would be able to keep his big toe.

'You're a very lucky boy,' his coach told him when he woke up after the surgery. 'Please don't play on that pitch ever again!'

After five weeks of rest, Stevie was able to play football again. Those were the most boring weeks of his life. The only good things were that he missed lots of school and he watched lots of football on TV.

When he returned to Liverpool Academy, Stevie worked really hard to get back to fitness. Football was the most important thing in the world to him, and after nearly losing his toe, he was more determined than ever.

'Stevie, it's just a practice,' the coaches shouted at him. 'Go easy on your teammates!'

He needed to calm down before he injured himself or someone else.

'You can't tackle like that all the time,' Steve Heighway told him. 'You've got to learn to control yourself and know when to dive in. We know how competitive you are but if you're not careful, you'll get hurt or sent off.'

Stevie listened carefully to his coaches. He was always keen to learn new things, even when everything was going well. The Liverpool Under-12s were winning every week. Stevie and Michael were the perfect partnership in attack – neither of them very tall for their age but with the pace, confidence and talent to beat much bigger teams. Every time Stevie played a great pass, Michael would score.

'It's great to have you back!' Michael said as they celebrated another goal.

Every summer, Liverpool sent out letters to the players that they wanted to come back for the next season. Even though Stevie was one of its rising stars, it was a nervous wait for him.

'There's no need for you to worry,' Steve reassured him at the end of one training session. 'You're going to be our captain.'

Stevie couldn't wait to tell his family the great news. He was the new leader of Liverpool Boys.

'Congratulations son, we're so proud of you!' his dad said when Stevie got home.

'Are you sure they were talking about the right player?' Paul joked with him. He always liked to wind up his younger brother. 'It must be a very bad team!'

Stevie laughed. The future was looking very bright indeed.

CHAPTER 8

LIVERPOOL VS. LILLESHALL

'Come in, lads,' Steve Heighway shouted through the door at the Liverpool training ground.

Stevie was standing outside with Michael Owen and two other teammates, Stephen Wright and Neil Murphy. Sometimes it was bad news if you got called to the coach's office but today the four of them were hoping for some really good news.

'Well done boys,' Steve Heighway said, 'you've been invited to trials at Lilleshall!'

Stevie couldn't believe it. Lilleshall was the National School where the top young English footballers went for the best coaching. Every kid dreamed of going to Lilleshall – there was no better place to develop as a player. Now Stevie, Wrighty and Michael would have the chance to be selected.

'It's going to be so competitive but we can do it,' Michael said with lots of confidence.

'You're right – we play for Liverpool, the best team in England!' Stevie shouted with a huge smile on his face.

There were many highly talented youngsters at the trials but both Stevie and Michael sailed through each round. Hundreds of hopefuls were reduced to fifty, then to twenty-four, but they were both still there. It was really hard work but they believed in themselves.

'I don't think there are any better strikers here but I hope they don't think I'm too small,' Michael said.

'When you're that quick and that good at shooting, it doesn't matter how tall you are!' Stevie replied. 'In midfield, there are some big, strong boys but I'm the best passer and the best tackler.'

'I've never seen anyone so brave!' Michael added.

Stevie was very impatient as he waited for the Lilleshall letter to arrive. Just one final trial awaited him, and he was desperate to get the invitation.

Every day, he ran out of the house to meet the postman, hoping for good news.

'Has the letter arrived?' Stevie asked, out of breath.

'Sorry, lad – not today,' the postman replied.

One day, the Lilleshall letter arrived and Paul Sr opened it. Stevie waited at the top of the stairs with his fingers firmly crossed. There was a pause as his dad read the letter.

'What does it say?' Stevie asked impatiently.

There was a sad look on his dad's face. Stevie knew that it was bad news – Lilleshall had rejected him. He ran back upstairs and slammed his bedroom door. He cried and cried, punching his pillow in anger. He was the captain of Liverpool Boys and the best young midfielder in England. How could they crush his dream like that?

Eventually, Paul Sr came up to comfort his son.

'Dad, I'm finished – I don't want to play football anymore!' Stevie said without looking up.

'I'm sorry, son – they've made a mistake,' Paul Sr said, giving his son a hug. 'You're a very good footballer and you did so well to get this far. I don't know why they turned you down, but now you have to show them why they should have picked you. Don't give up.'

Michael was chosen for Lilleshall, which made it all the harder to bear for Stevie. He was pleased for his friend but it still really hurt. Back at Liverpool, Steve Heighway tried to lift the boy's spirits. 'I know you're very upset but I'm so pleased that you're not going to Lilleshall. You're my superstar and I promise you that I can make you a better player than they can.'

Stevie was determined to prove Lilleshall wrong. His journey to the top might be more difficult at Liverpool but nothing could stop him. Seven months later, The National School came to play a match. Stevie couldn't wait.

'Those Lilleshall boys, they think they're better than you,' Paul Sr told his son the night before, to get him pumped up for the big game. But Stevie didn't need any more encouragement; he was ready for the biggest match of his life.

From the first whistle, Stevie flew into tackle after

tackle. The Lilleshall midfield faced a considerable challenge. The referee asked Stevie to calm down but he wasn't listening. Lilleshall won 4–3, with Michael scoring a hat-trick, but Stevie – for Liverpool – had played the best match of his career so far.

'Well played,' the Lilleshall players said as they shook Stevie's hand at the end. They knew how good Stevie was and they were scared of him.

'It's a joke that they didn't select you,' Michael told him as they chatted after the game. 'You're so much better than the others!'

At Liverpool, Steve Heighway looked after Stevie like a son. With the right support, he was sure that his young captain would be a great player for his club and country. Steve took both Stevie and Michael on the Under-18 tour to Spain when they were still playing for the Under-14s.

'It's important for you to get these experiences as early as possible,' Steve told them. 'You're travelling with the team, representing Liverpool against top teams in Europe. You can learn a lot from just watching these games.'

Steve also secured Stevie tickets for Liverpool first team matches. Sometimes, Stevie went to Anfield with his brother but when The Reds made it to a big final, Stevie would travel to Wembley with Steve and his family.

'Liverpool are going to destroy Bolton today!' Stevie said on the train down to London. It was the 1995 Coca-Cola Cup Final and Liverpool, with great players like Jamie Redknapp, John Barnes, Steve McManaman, Ian Rush and Robbie Fowler, were the favourites to win.

As a fifteen-year-old from Huyton, Stevie loved being part of the big crowds heading to Wembley. The fans were all dressed up in their team's colours and everyone was singing songs. Looking up at the massive national stadium in front of him, he dreamed of one day playing there in front of 75,000 fans.

'You'll be out there soon,' Steve Heighway said as they took their seats, reading his mind. 'For Liverpool and for England!'

Liverpool played really well and they had lots of chances to score. With a few minutes left in the first half, McManaman dribbled through the middle. With three defenders in front of him, he used his pace to run around the outside. McManaman cut inside past the last defender and shot into the net.

'What a goal!' Stevie shouted as he celebrated with the other Liverpool fans.

In the second half, McManaman got the ball on the left and ran forward. He cut into the penalty area on his right foot, dribbled past a defender and curled the ball into the bottom corner.

'He's incredible!' Stevie screamed.

McManaman was eight years older than him but Stevie began to picture a future Liverpool team – Jamie Carragher in defence, Gerrard and Redknapp in the centre of midfield, with McManaman on the wing and Fowler and Owen up front. What a team that would be.

CHAPTER 9

PLAYING WITH THE BIG BOYS

The young Liverpool players had to do some work experience. Some of the boys worked at supermarkets or building sites, but Stevie had an alternative idea.

'The older boys told me that sometimes you can do the two weeks at Liverpool,' Stevie said to Steve Heighway. 'I want to do that! I'll do anything – clean boots, mop the floors.'

Steve agreed to sort this out for his star player. When Stevie arrived at Melwood, the Liverpool training ground, he was expecting to do boring tasks in the dressing room. But he was in for a surprise.

'Right, lad, you'll be helping with the first team training today,' one of the coaches told him.

Stevie couldn't believe it. Work experience kids had trained with the reserves in the past but this was even better. He stood on the touchline watching his hero John Barnes up close and it was the best thing he had ever seen. Barnes's skills were just amazing.

'We need another player for the five-a-side match,' the Liverpool manager, Roy Evans, told him, throwing him a yellow bib.

Stevie was speechless. He was sixteen years old and now he was passing the ball to Barnes. Was he dreaming? At the end of the game, Barnes gave him a pat on the back.

'Well played, kid,' he said and Stevie would never forget that moment. He couldn't wait to play with the big boys every day.

Lots of other clubs were taking an interest in Stevie, and he visited a few of them – Everton, Manchester United – to have a look around and play a few practice matches. At Manchester United, he met Alex Ferguson and they tried to sign him, but

Stevie just wanted Liverpool to offer him a contract. There was only one place that he wanted to play football.

'How was Old Trafford?' Steve Heighway asked when Stevie returned. There was no chance that he would let his star player sign for Manchester United.

'It was great,' the youth replied with smile. 'I'm thinking about their offer…'

'You were born to play here at Anfield,' Steve told him.

'I know but I don't have a contract yet…' Stevie said cheekily.

'Leave it with me – I'll get that sorted.'

A few weeks later, Stevie had a Youth Trainee Scheme contract. He would be paid £50 each week to become a professional footballer. He was so proud to sign for the club that he had supported all his life – and his family were delighted too.

'Our son, the Liverpool player!' Paul Sr said at dinner, lifting his glass to raise a toast.

'At this rate, you'll be the smallest player ever to play at Anfield,' Paul Jr joked.

Once he had finished his exams, Stevie started
his apprenticeship at Liverpool. Every time he put
on the red club shirt, he felt on top of the world.
It was the happiest time of his life. Together with
friends like Michael, he worked hard and played
hard.

As one of the players walked into the dressing
room, Michael nodded and Stevie quickly turned the
lights off. In the darkness, they flicked their towels at
their teammate over and over again.

Owwwwwwww! Stop it!

Hahahahahahahahahaha!

Off the pitch, they were always making fun of
each other's clothes but on the pitch, they were a
great team. Stevie loved the competitive atmosphere.
Everyone always gave 110 per cent.

Training sessions took place at Melwood,
right next to the Liverpool first team. Redknapp,
McManaman, Fowler and David James were the
big stars and they always looked cool. Stevie tried
to speak to them whenever he could. He wasn't
nervous around them; he wanted to be part of

their gang. All of the young players tried to copy everything 'The Spice Boys' did.

One day after training, Jamie Redknapp came over to Stevie. Normally, the senior players only spoke to the young players if they wanted them to get something for them.

'You're a very good player,' Jamie said. 'You're passing is really good and that shot is powerful. Keep it up!'

Stevie was so happy to hear an England international praising him. After that, Jamie often offered him advice about how to be a better midfielder. Stevie listened carefully to every single word.

'Have these,' Jamie said to him one day in the dressing room, and threw him a brand new pair of Mizuno boots. Stevie cleaned Jamie's boots every week and they were the nicest that he had ever seen. He couldn't wait to wear them.

'Thanks, Jamie!' Stevie said with a big smile on his face.

The only problem in those days was the risk of

injuries. Stevie had grown suddenly from a little kid to six feet tall, and his body was struggling to cope with the changes. Sometimes his ankles were sore but he felt most pain in his back and knees. Every time he was playing well, the injuries would return.

'How are you feeling?' the Liverpool physio asked him, touching the different parts of his knees.

Stevie winced with the pain. 'It's not getting any better – this is so frustrating!'

One day when things were really bad, the manager Roy Evans spoke to him. 'I know this is a tough time for you but you have to keep your head up and keep working hard. Everyone here at Liverpool thinks very highly of you. As soon as you get these injuries sorted, you'll be up in the first team, I'm sure.'

Stevie was really pleased to hear that from the Liverpool manager. Sometimes he was unlucky with injuries but sometimes, he just needed to be more sensible, especially in training. He loved to tackle but there was no point in hurting himself just to impress.

'How many times have we told you to calm down?' said Ronnie Moran, one of the Liverpool coaches. 'You're flying into big tackles when you've just come back from injury!'

With the club starting to offer professional contracts to his teammates, Stevie was getting very worried. Liverpool wanted to see him in fit and healthy form, but what if the injuries never went away?

'Dad, this uncertainty is awful!' he complained.

So Paul Sr went to see Steve Heighway. 'As you know, Stevie is really struggling at the moment. All of this contract talk is really affecting his performances. You know how much he wants this – can't we just get it sorted now?'

Steve spoke to Roy Evans, and soon Stevie Gerrard had his first professional contract. It was the best day of his life as he signed the papers. It was the start of great times at Liverpool.

CHAPTER 10

ANOTHER STEP CLOSER

With his contract signed, Stevie got back to doing what he did best – passing the ball, tackling players and scoring goals from midfield. With Jamie's advice in his head, he ran from box to box and never stopped. He was doing well for the Liverpool Under-19s and everyone was talking about him.

'They say that Tottenham want to buy you for £2 million!' said Stephen Wright, or 'Wrighty' as most of the squad called him, at training one day.

It was just a rumour but that was a lot of money for a youngster who had never before played for the first team. Stevie didn't even think about leaving

Liverpool but it was nice to hear that he was attracting attention.

One morning as he arrived for training, Steve Heighway asked him to come into his office.

'Stevie, you'll have people watching you this morning,' he warned. 'Sammy Lee and Patrice Bergues are coming down to see you in action. Don't panic – just play your natural game.'

Two of the top Liverpool coaches were coming to watch him – this was the biggest day of his life. The new manager, Gérard Houllier had just arrived from France and he wanted to bring more young players into the first team squad. This was like a trial and Stevie was ready to shine.

He worked harder than ever, winning every ball and playing perfect passes. Most of all, Stevie tried to take up good positions to receive the ball, and to look calm in possession. Those were the qualities that he needed to display to make the next step up. He could see Sammy and Patrice on the touchline, chatting and taking notes. Sweat was pouring down Stevie's face but he kept going right until the end of the session.

As Stevie walked off the pitch, Steve introduced him to Patrice and Sammy.

'Well done, you looked good today,' Sammy said, shaking his hand, and Patrice nodded in agreement.

Stevie couldn't help smiling. He was impressing the right people at the club. Hopefully, Houllier himself would come to watch him soon.

One day, as Stevie warmed up against Manchester United, he saw Houllier standing with the other Liverpool coaches. He took a deep breath – this needed to be his best match yet. With his tough tackling, Stevie won the battle against the United midfield and he showed that he could create lots of chances with his passing too. He capped off a great performance with a powerful strike from the edge of the penalty area. As he celebrated the goal, Stevie looked to the bench but Houllier was gone. He just hoped that the manager had seen enough.

'Did you know Houllier was there today?' Paul Sr asked as he drove Stevie home from the game.

'Of course!' he said with a smile.

'Well, you did very well today, kid,' his dad replied.

A few days later, Steve Heighway called Stevie and Wrighty into his office. 'I've got big news for you, lads. Houllier wants you to train with the first team at Melwood from now on. You start on Monday.'

Stevie and Wrighty looked at each other and smiled. This was it.

'This is a big chance for you,' Steve continued, 'but I want you to always remember your days here in the Academy. You'll need to keep your feet on the ground over the next few months. You're not a Liverpool first team footballer yet.'

Stevie nodded. He was very grateful for all of Steve's guidance over the years and he would always listen to his first coach's advice. Moving to Melwood was only the start – there was plenty of work still to be done.

'Congratulations mate, welcome to the first team!' Jamie said as Stevie arrived in the dressing room. He was nervous and he didn't want to sit in someone else's seat. He looked around for his name but it wasn't written anywhere.

'Over there!' one of the coaches pointed and Stevie sat down in the far corner next to the big bag of footballs. He wasn't one of the big boys yet.

It was the hardest training session that Stevie had endured, but he enjoyed every second of it. He loved to challenge himself and players like McManaman and Fowler were the best around. When practice finished, Houllier asked Stevie and Wrighty to stay behind.

'You're both good players but you need to get bigger and stronger,' the manager told them. 'Right now, you look tiny next to the other players but we'll help you to get to their level. Just listen carefully and don't complain.'

For the first time in his life, Stevie began to think about his diet. He didn't eat lots of fast food but he stopped eating burgers altogether. Instead, he ate more pasta and salads. Stevie needed to get really serious about football, and – as they kept telling him, 'live like an athlete'.

'This is so boring!' Wrighty said, as he rested after lifting weights in the club gym. Every day, the pair did football training in the morning and then strength training in the afternoon. It was really hard work but Stevie was focused on achieving his goals.

'Next time you lift that bar, picture standing in the tunnel for your Liverpool debut,' Stevie told Wrighty. 'That's what I do. I imagine myself touching the "This is Anfield" sign with the noise of fans all around me. It will be the best day of our lives and every weights session gets us closer to that day.'

In November 1998, Liverpool were playing in the UEFA Cup and for their third round match against Celta Vigo, Houllier invited Stevie and Wrighty to travel with the squad.

'We're going to Spain!' Wrighty cheered loudly.

They didn't expect to play in the game but it would be a great experience to be around the first team players. Stevie shared a hotel room with Jamie Redknapp and continued to learn from him. He watched what he did, what he said and what he ate. There was so much to learn.

On the day of the match, Stevie walked into the dressing room and there was a shirt with his name on it – '28 GERRARD'. He couldn't believe it. He was going to be a Liverpool substitute. Only a month earlier, he had been playing for the Under-19s.

Liverpool lost 3–1 and Stevie didn't actually get to play, but he learnt a lot from the game. Claude Makélélé was the defensive midfielder for Celta Vigo and he calmly controlled the match, passing forward to his more skilful teammates. He made it look so easy. It was the kind of neat, possession football that Stevie wanted to excel at. Now, he was getting so close to that Liverpool debut.

CHAPTER 11

THE DEBUT

'Incey, you better watch out – Stevie's going to take your place!' Jamie joked in training.

Paul Ince was Jamie's partner in central midfield and he was an England international. But Stevie was fearless and he was doing everything he could to win his Liverpool debut.

For Liverpool's Premier League match against Blackburn in November 1998, Stevie was included in the eighteen-man squad for the very first time. It was great news but he didn't get excited until he made the final sixteen.

'Houllier thinks you can play central midfield, right-back or right midfield,' Jamie said to him. 'That makes you a great substitute to have. Be ready to come on!'

Liverpool were winning 2–0 and Houllier sent the subs out to warm up along the touchline. The atmosphere was brilliant at Anfield and the fans clapped them as they ran along and did some stretches. Did they know who Stevie was? He doubted it; to them, he was probably a skinny kid who would never make it to the top.

'I'll show them,' he said to himself.

With a few minutes to go, Stevie thought he would have to wait another week for his debut. But then Sammy Lee called his name.

'You're coming on, lad!'

As he stood on the touchline, Stevie tucked his shirt in and tried to stay calm. His heart was beating so fast. This was the moment that he had been dreaming about for years.

'Good luck, kid!' teammate Phil Thompson said. 'You'll be playing at right-back.'

'Keep the ball, there's not long to go,' Houllier told him.

When the ball came to Stevie, he controlled it carefully and played a simple pass to another teammate. The relief was incredible. He hadn't made a mistake with his first touches. A few seconds later, Incey played a ball to him down the wing. Stevie had a great chance to cross the ball into the box. It was something he had done so many times before but this was different. With the pressure on, he put far too much power on the cross and it sailed out for a goal kick. The Liverpool fans groaned.

'Sorry!' he shouted to his teammates.

When the referee blew the final whistle, Stevie relaxed. Now, he could finally enjoy his big day.

'Well done, mate. How was that?' Michael said, as they hugged on the pitch.

'I've never been so nervous,' Stevie admitted. 'Incey won't let me forget that awful cross for years!'

Michael had made his first team debut at seventeen, and now Stevie had done it at eighteen. They were the future of Liverpool Football Club and it was so exciting.

All of his teammates congratulated Stevie in the dressing room, especially Jamie. Now, he really felt like part of the team. As soon as he was changed, he went out into the players' lounge to see his family.

'Well done, son!' Paul Sr shouted as soon as he saw him.

'What was that cross about?' Paul Jr joked.

Even his brother's teasing couldn't take the smile off Stevie's face. He was officially a Liverpool first team footballer now and that was the best feeling in the world.

A week later, Stevie started in the match against Tottenham. He had hoped to play in his favourite central midfield role this time but when he saw the team sheet, he saw that he was at right-back again. And against Spurs, that meant a very difficult opponent – David Ginola. Ginola was a really skilful winger and he was much stronger than Stevie too. He tried really hard to tackle him but the Frenchman was just too good. Stevie was having a nightmare match and he wanted it to be over.

'Keep going!' Jamie shouted to him.

By the end of the match, Stevie thought his Liverpool career was over. Surely Houllier would decide that he wasn't good enough for the first team. But instead, the manager came up to him and patted him on the back.

'That was a very tough game but you did okay,' Houllier said to him. 'You didn't give up and you showed the character that we're looking for.'

It felt great to have so much support from the players and coaches. There was a real family atmosphere at Liverpool and Stevie loved it. Everyone believed in him and, with every minute he was on the pitch, he was learning so much.

When Jamie got injured, Stevie finally got the chance to play in central midfield. He felt much more comfortable in his normal position, running up and down through the centre of the pitch. He had so much energy and he wasn't afraid of anything. Against Middlesbrough, he was up against one of his childhood heroes, Paul Gascoigne. He could remember watching him at Euro 96 on TV back on the Bluebell Estate. In the first minute of this match, though, Gazza ran into him and hit him right in the face.

'Owwwwwwwww!' Stevie screamed. His face was throbbing with pain. He would have a great black eye in the morning.

He was only a youngster and Gazza was an England legend but Stevie flew into the next tackle. Gazza skipped past him but the game became a battle between the two of them. Liverpool won and at the end of the match, Gazza approached him.

'You're a really good player,' he said, putting an arm around Stevie. 'Keep playing like that and you'll be a star.'

That was the best thing Stevie had ever heard. He couldn't wait to tell his family; his brother would be so jealous.

By the end of the 1998–99 season, Stevie had played in twelve Premier League matches and a few European games too. He was having the time of his life and the fans were chanting his name.

'Next year, my aim is to become Houllier's first choice in central midfield,' he told Michael.

'What about Incey and Jamie?' his friend asked.

'What about them?!' Stevie replied. He was full of confidence.

CHAPTER 12

BOX TO BOX

'What did I tell you?' Stevie said to Michael with a smile. Incey had been sold to Middlesbrough in the summer of 1999 and Stevie was now Jamie's regular partner in midfield. While Jamie played the nice passes and set up goals, Stevie ran everywhere and did lots of tackling.

'Yes, you were right about that,' Michael said, 'but are you ever going to score any goals? You used to take lots of shots for the youth team but now you hardly ever cross the halfway line.'

His friend was right; Stevie needed to show the Liverpool coaches that he could really attack as well as defend. With his pace, he could burst forward from midfield and help out the strikers. But if he ever got into good positions, he panicked and passed the ball, or shot high over the bar.

'All I need is that first goal,' Stevie explained to Michael. 'Once I have that, I think I'll feel much more confident.'

At home to Sheffield Wednesday in December 1999, Liverpool were 2–0 up with twenty minutes to go. With Jamie injured, Didi Hamann was playing in defensive midfield and Stevie was told to push forward. This was his chance to show what he could do.

Stevie ran quickly towards the heart of the Sheffield Wednesday defence. They weren't ready for his pace and he glided past one man and then another. He was in the penalty area with only the goalkeeper to beat. This was when he needed to stay calm. He imagined that he was still back at Happy Street, pretending to be John Barnes with his mates. His shot was low and hard, and right into the bottom corner of the net.

Goooooooooooooooooaaaaaaaaaaaaaaaaaaaaaaaaaaa aalllllllllllllllllllllllllllllllllllll!!!!

Stevie had done it! He slid along the grass towards the fans and his teammates jumped on top of him. He could hear the fans chanting his name. Nothing could beat that feeling.

'What a run!' Didi shouted. 'I didn't know you could dribble like that.'

Suddenly, Stevie wasn't just a tough tackler; he was an attacker too. If they beat Arsenal, Liverpool could climb to third in the table. Again, Didi played slightly deeper and Houllier asked Stevie to be more creative.

After fifteen minutes of the Arsenal game, Stevie secured the ball in his own half. As he looked up, he saw Titi Camara making a brilliant run behind the Arsenal defence. Stevie would need to deliver an amazing pass, but he had been famous for his long passes in the Liverpool youth team. This was the perfect time to see if he could do it at the highest level.

So he curled the ball past the Arsenal defenders and straight into Titi's path. The striker ran towards goal and shot past the keeper, David Seaman. Liverpool were winning.

In the second half, the Arsenal midfielder Freddie Ljungberg ran through on goal. He took the ball around the goalkeeper and he looked certain to score the equaliser. But just as he was about to shoot, Stevie ran in and made a brilliant tackle. When the final whistle went, Stevie was the match-winner.

'That's one of the best performances I've ever seen,' Didi said as they celebrated with the fans.

Stevie was really pleased with the way that he was developing as a player. He was an all-round midfielder now who could tackle, pass, *and* shoot. He was a regular for the England Under-21 team but there were rumours that the senior England manager, Kevin Keegan, was watching him too.

'You'd be great with Paul Scholes in midfield,' Michael Owen said excitedly. After his brilliant goals at World Cup 1998, Michael was a regular for the England team and he wanted his friend Stevie playing with him.

One day, Paul Jr called Stevie and told him to phone Steve Heighway.

'What's going on?' asked Stevie.

'Congratulations, kid,' Steve told him happily. 'Keegan wants you to go and train with the England squad before the friendly against Argentina.'

Stevie was so excited. He understood that he wouldn't play in the match but it was a big step forward just to be around the team. If he did well in the practices, perhaps he would be called up to the next squad.

As he drove to the training camp, Stevie got more and more nervous. He was only nineteen years old and he would be joining really experienced, world-class players like Sol Campbell, David Beckham and Alan Shearer. Was he good enough, though? When he arrived at the hotel, Stevie called Jamie who was already downstairs at dinner.

'Mate, can you help me please?' he said. 'I'm really worried about making a fool of myself.'

Jamie ran upstairs. 'Come on, there's nothing to worry about. Keegan called you up because he thinks you're good enough,' he said, pushing Stevie towards the stairs. 'I think you're good enough, Michael thinks you're good enough, Robbie thinks you're good enough – so you're good enough!'

Keegan introduced Stevie to all of the players. The youth could barely stand up because he was shaking so much, but he soon felt more at ease as everyone was really friendly. On the training field, he loved how competitive everyone was. There were lots of tough tackles and arguments.

The talent was a joy to watch. Shearer could score in the top corner every time; Beckham could cross the ball perfectly on to the striker's head; and Scholes could always see space before everyone else and play a really clever pass. Stevie had a long way to go to reach their level but he would do everything he could to get there.

One day, in May 2000, as he walked through Liverpool with his dad, Stevie's phone rang.

'Hello?'

'Hi Stevie, this is Kevin Keegan,' the voice on the other end said.

At first, he thought it was a teammate playing a joke but soon, Stevie realised that it really was Keegan calling.

'I'm calling you up for the game on Wednesday,' the England Manager told him, and Stevie felt like dancing through the city streets. 'See you at the team hotel.'

England's opponents would be Ukraine. At the training camp, Stevie worked hard and just hoped that he would get to play. Keegan came over to talk to him on the day before the game.

'Are you excited about tomorrow night?' he asked.

'Of course, I can't wait!' Stevie replied.

'Good, because you're starting,' Keegan said.

Stevie couldn't believe it. He'd be playing in midfield with Beckham, Scholes and McManaman. That was a terrifying thought. The next twenty-four hours went by very slowly. Stevie just wanted to get out onto the pitch and make his England debut.

In the dressing room, Stevie had never heard so much passion and shouting before a match. It was the best atmosphere ever and it only got better as they came out of the tunnel.

For eighty minutes, Stevie ran and ran across the beautiful Wembley grass. Ukraine had great players like Andriy Shevchenko but he didn't let them have time on the ball. Stevie made some good tackles and he ran forward to support the strikers when he could. It wasn't a spectacular debut but it was a solid one. As he left the pitch, the England fans clapped and cheered.

'Well played, lad,' Keegan said as he went to sit down on the bench.

Stevie just hoped that he had done enough to make the England squad for Euro 2000.

CHAPTER 13

AN AMAZING YEAR

'I'm in – I'm coming to Belgium and Holland with you!' Stevie told Michael. Having just turned twenty years old, this was beyond Stevie's wildest dreams. He couldn't wait for their big Euro 2000 adventure to begin.

As he arrived at the England camp, Stevie was full of high hopes for the tournament but a few days later, he really missed home. He had never been away for so long before.

'Why don't you speak to your parents?' Michael suggested. 'I find it always helps to hear a friendly voice and talk about family things. You'll be back in Liverpool in no time.'

His teammates were really kind and invited him to play snooker and card games with them. Once he was working really hard to impress the coaches, he had no time to feel homesick. Portugal had world-class attackers like Rui Costa and Luís Figo, and he knew that Incey and Scholesy had lots more experience of playing in big matches. Stevie watched from the bench as England lost 3–2.

It meant that they would need a victory in their next game. Early in the second half against Germany, Alan Shearer headed the ball into the net. 1–0! Ten minutes later, Keegan made a substitution to protect the lead.

'Stevie, go and get warmed up!' one of the coaches shouted and his heart started beating a lot faster.

His job was to come on and make lots of tackles to try and stop the Germans from scoring. There was a lot of pressure on Stevie but tackling was what he was born to do. He warmed up every muscle in his body – he was ready for the challenge.

As he ran on, Stevie listened to the incredible

noise of the England fans. He was nervous but he was also looking forward to the battle. He raced around the pitch, blocking passes and stopping attacks. He vowed that no-one was getting past him. By the final whistle, the atmosphere was incredible. England had beaten Germany.

'Congratulations, mate,' Didi Hamann, Stevie's teammate at Liverpool, said as they swapped shirts. 'You played really well.'

'What a performance, lad!' Keegan said, giving Stevie a big hug.

It felt so good to be part of the victory. The next day, the national newspapers called Stevie 'England's future' and 'an England captain in the making'. It was a very proud moment.

Keegan wanted his new star to play in the last group match against Romania but Stevie had hurt his calf in the Germany match. Without him, England lost 3–2 and crashed out of the tournament. It was a very disappointing end but Stevie was excited about the next Premier League season.

It was great to be back in Liverpool. Houllier was

building a strong team, with Sami Hyypiä and Jamie Carragher in defence, Didi and Stevie in midfield and Michael, Emile Heskey and Robbie Fowler up front. When Scottish midfielder Gary McAllister signed from Coventry, everyone was surprised.

'Why have we bought him? He's old!' Stevie said at training when they heard the news.

But Macca was very experienced and Stevie learnt a lot from listening to him, especially about calmly picking the best pass. Stevie sometimes had so much energy that he moved too fast without thinking.

'Be smarter with the ball,' Macca advised him again and again. 'Keep possession – if you can't play a good long pass, play a safe short pass instead.'

With great players and coaches around him, Stevie was getting better and better. After Euro 2000, he was determined to live up to the hype. Sometimes he still got too angry in big matches but he was scoring more goals and Liverpool were playing well in all competitions. In February 2001, they won the League Cup and in May, they made it to two more finals.

First came the FA Cup Final against Arsenal. The Gunners took the lead after seventy minutes.

'Come on, we've got to keep going,' Stevie told his teammates as they stood around with their heads down. He was still young but he was showing clear signs of leadership. 'It's not over yet!'

Macca crossed a free-kick into the box and Michael smashed the ball into the net. The game was heading for extra time but Patrik Berger played a beautiful long pass for Michael to run on to. He was far too quick for the Arsenal defenders and he calmly slotted the ball past the goalkeeper. At the final whistle, the Liverpool players hugged each other. It was an amazing team victory over a brilliant Arsenal side.

'Right, we've won the double,' Stevie said to Michael once he had kissed the cup. 'Now for the treble!'

Having reached the UEFA Cup Final, Liverpool were favourites to beat the Spanish side Alavés. After fifteen minutes, Michael got the ball in attack and Stevie made a brilliant run from midfield. When the pass arrived, he took one touch and calmly struck the ball into the bottom corner.

Goooooooooooooooooaaaaaaaaaaaaaaaaaaaaallllllllllll llllllllllllllllllllllllllllll!!!!!!!!!!!!

Stevie and Michael celebrated another great Liverpool team goal with the fans. At half-time, Liverpool were leading 3–1 but in the second half, the Spanish team began to catch up. The score was 4–4 after ninety minutes. It had been a very exciting game and the players were exhausted.

'We don't want this to go to penalties,' Stevie told his teammates as they sat on the grass and stretched their legs. 'Let's get a winner in extra time.'

With three minutes to go, Alavés scored an own goal. It was a cruel way to lose but Liverpool had their third trophy of the season. As Robbie and Sami lifted the trophy, red confetti flew up into the night air and Stevie jumped up and down with his teammates.

What an amazing season it had been. Stevie had three winners' medals and he was named the PFA Young Player of the Year too. Could it get any better?

'Next up, The Premier League title and the Champions League!' he told Michael.

CHAPTER 14

CAPTAIN OF LIVERPOOL

Stevie signed a big new contract at Liverpool. 'This is my home!' he told the fans happily.

Everything was going so well for him but one problem remained – he had to stop getting sent off for dangerous tackles.

'That was really stupid,' Macca told him after another red card against Aston Villa. Stevie had let his team down and he felt very ashamed. 'When you get frustrated, you can't just do that. You have to think about when to tackle hard and when to take a deep breath and walk away.'

'You're my vice-captain now,' Houllier told Stevie, 'and so you have to lead by example.' The player could hear the disappointment in his manager's voice. 'You'll be a great Liverpool captain soon,' Houllier went on, 'but only if you calm down on the pitch.'

Stevie listened to all of the advice and began to learn from his mistakes. He was still young but there were no excuses for his behaviour. Aggression and bravery were very important parts of his playing style but if he didn't learn to control his temper, he could hurt other players and he could hurt himself too. As a result of a groin injury, he had to miss the 2002 World Cup in South Korea and Japan.

'I can't keep playing like this,' Stevie said to himself.

He was really upset to be watching the tournament on TV. He had played a key role in England's great qualifying campaign, notably at the Olympiastadion in Munich. Germany had taken the lead after six minutes but Michael scored an equaliser. In the last minute of the first half, a Beckham cross was headed out to Stevie, who was at least thirty yards from goal.

Stevie had nothing to lose. He chested the ball down and struck a powerful shot. The ball flew through the air, bounced and then zipped along into the bottom corner. The goalkeeper had no chance.

Goooooooooooooooooooooooaaaaaaaaaaaaaaaaaa aaaaaallllllllllllllllllllllllllllll!!!!!!

It was Stevie's first goal for England – and what a goal it was. He ran towards the corner flag and then dived along the grass. His teammates were right behind him and jumped on top of him.

'What a shot!'

'That's a worldie!'

The game finished 5–1 to England, with Michael scoring a hat-trick. It was one of the best days of Stevie's life.

Now, Stevie focused on getting fit for the new Premier League season. He needed to show that he was more mature now.

Liverpool weren't playing well in the Premiership but they were through to the League Cup Final again. This time, they were up against massive rivals Manchester United. Stevie couldn't wait.

'There's nothing like beating United!' he told Michael in the dressing room before kick-off. 'When I was a young Liverpool fan, they were always the games I wanted to win most. Now, I get to play and win the games myself!'

As the first half came to an end, Stevie got the ball about thirty yards out. That first England goal had shown the fans that he was brilliant at shooting from long range. They wanted to see another great strike.

Shoot! Shoot!

Beckham ran out to close him down but Stevie's shot deflected off his leg and rocketed into the top corner. In his excitement, Stevie took his shirt off and ran towards the fans. In the biggest match of their season, he had scored the first goal.

Stevie ran and ran to stop the Manchester United attacks. Jerzy Dudek made some great saves but Liverpool still needed a second goal. On the counter-attack, Didi played a great pass to Michael and he shot past Fabien Barthez.

'That's it – we've won!' Stevie shouted, giving Michael a big hug.

It felt so good to beat Manchester United, especially in a cup final. It was another winner's medal for Stevie but it wasn't the one that he really wanted.

'We're great in cup competitions but why can't we do well over thirty-eight matches in the Premier League?' he asked Michael.

'We need to be more consistent,' Michael replied. 'We have to win the less important games too.'

They both loved Liverpool Football Club but the team needed to change their way of thinking in order to reach the next level. It was all about belief and the desire to win. Stevie and Michael had these qualities but did all of the others?

Houllier was thinking about changes too.

'Come and see me after training,' he said to Stevie as they got ready for the season ahead.

In his office, Houllier was sitting with his assistant, Phil Thompson. 'Stevie, we've been talking to the coaches and a few of the players and we've decided to try a new captain,' Houllier explained. 'We think you're ready to take on the responsibility.'

Stevie couldn't believe it – it was a massive honour for a twenty-three-year-old, especially one who was a local lad and a big Liverpool fan. He had always dreamt of being the club captain, leading his team out onto the pitch at Anfield.

'Thanks, I won't let the club down!' he told Houllier with a big smile on his face.

CHAPTER 15

THINKING ABOUT THE FUTURE

'We've got a great chance at this tournament,'
Stevie said to Michael as they made their way to
Portugal for Euro 2004. 'This is our best squad
for years!'

David Beckham, Scholesy and Sol Campbell were
experienced, older players and there were lots of
very good younger players too like Frank Lampard,
John Terry, Wayne Rooney, Stevie and Michael.
Everyone got on really well and there were lots of
practical jokes and card games to amuse them while
they waited for the tournament to begin.

England's first match was against a France team
featuring Zinedine Zidane, Thierry Henry and Patrick

Vieira. They would have to be on top form to beat the French.

'They're good but we've got nothing to fear,' Beckham told his teammates in the dressing room before kick-off. 'We're as good as anyone – let's make our country proud!'

The players roared like lions and prepared for battle. The atmosphere in the stadium was amazing. Stevie looked up and there seemed to be England fans everywhere, waving their white flags with the red cross of St George. Frank scored a header in the first half and even when Beckham missed a penalty, it looked like England would get a great first win.

In the last few minutes of the match, though, France won a free-kick. Zidane stepped up and hit a perfect shot into the corner of the net. The England players were disappointed but a draw would be a good result.

'Keep your heads up, boys,' Becks shouted. 'We just need to hold on for a few more minutes.'

The ball came to Stevie and he tried to play it back to the goalkeeper, David James. But he hadn't seen Henry's clever run to intercept the pass. Stevie watched in horror as Henry beat James to the ball and the goalkeeper brought him down. Penalty! Zidane scored to win the match for France.

'Don't worry,' Michael said to Stevie. In the dressing room, he was silent, thinking about how he had let the team down with that awful error. 'Forget about it and move on to the next match.'

Against Switzerland, Wayne scored two great goals and then Stevie got a third. It was a relief to help his country towards victory this time.

'I think they've forgiven you!' Michael joked as the England supporters cheered Stevie's goal loudly.

England made it through to the quarter-finals against Portugal. As hosts of the tournament, Portugal had a massive swell of home support, and their team's wingers, Luis Figo and Cristiano Ronaldo, were very skilful.

'We can do this!' Becks shouted in the dressing room and the players echoed his belief. This was their chance to shine. After thirty-eight years, it was time for England to win another trophy.

They had the perfect start when Michael scored in the third minute but then Wayne Rooney got injured. With England's star player off the pitch, the opposition grew more and more confident.

'Keep going, lads!' Stevie shouted as he chased after Portugal's skilful midfielders with sweat pouring down his face. He worked so hard in the summer heat that with ten minutes to go, Stevie had to come off. Only a minute later, Portugal equalised.

As he sat on the bench, Stevie held his head in his hands. He was so nervous that he could barely watch the match. In extra time, Portugal took the lead but Frank Lampard scored to take the match to penalties.

'Come on, you can do this!' Stevie said, patting everyone on the back. Normally, he would have been one of the takers and he wished that he could take one now.

After twelve penalties, it was 5–5. The tension was incredible. The whole team stood together on the halfway line to watch. They were into sudden death and when Darius Vassell's shot was saved, the Portuguese goalkeeper scored to win the match.

It was so disappointing to lose, especially on penalties. There were tears in everyone's eyes and no-one knew what to say. It was a very sad, quiet dressing room after the game but Wayne raised everyone's spirits.

'Don't worry, boys – that was just the warm-up for the 2006 World Cup!'

As Stevie returned to Liverpool, he thought long and hard about his future. He loved his local club but he was very ambitious. He wanted to be challenging for the Premiership and the Champions League. There were three big English clubs – Arsenal, Manchester United and Chelsea – and Liverpool lay a long way behind them.

'We finished thirty points behind Arsenal last season,' he said to his dad. 'That's just not good enough.'

'I know, son, but why don't you give Rafa one season to change your mind?' Paul Sr suggested.

Rafa Benitez had become the new manager of Liverpool in 2004 and the players were very excited to have such a big name in charge.

'He's a top coach,' Jamie Carragher said. 'His teams are strong, fit and very skilful. Every time we've played Valencia, they've destroyed us!'

Rafa had won the Spanish league twice in three years with Valencia, as well as the UEFA Cup. He was a winner and that's what Stevie and Liverpool needed.

Rafa visited Stevie, Michael and Carra at the England camp in Portugal. He said: 'I firmly believe that I can bring success to Liverpool but I need my best players to believe in me and work hard for me.'

Stevie was impressed by Rafa's plans for the club but meanwhile Chelsea were trying really hard to sign him. In Portugal, Frank Lampard and John Terry kept telling him about life at Stamford Bridge.

'It's the best! With Abramovich as chairman and Mourinho as manager, there's lots of money for new signings and we're going to win every trophy around,' Frank told Stevie confidently.

It was a very tempting offer but Stevie's family were desperate for him to stay at Liverpool.

'You've got to stay,' Paul Jr told his brother. 'You'll

hate it in London and Rafa's about to turn Liverpool into a quality side.'

In the end, Stevie decided to stay but he wanted to see improvements at Liverpool.

'You've made the right decision,' Rafa told him, patting him on the back. 'Together, we'll bring lots more trophies to Anfield.'

CHAPTER 16

CHAMPIONS OF EUROPE

'These new signings are really good!' Carra said after a pre-season training session.

Rafa had signed Djibril Cissé, a powerful new French striker, and two creative Spanish midfielders, Xabi Alonso and Luis García. Stevie was starting to get excited about the future of Liverpool Football Club.

But as the 2004–05 season was just about to start, Stevie got some bad news. Michael had been quiet for a few weeks and Rafa left him on the bench for the Champions League qualifier.

'What's going on?' Stevie asked. He was worried about his friend and teammate.

Michael couldn't keep the secret any longer. 'Real

Madrid have made a great offer for me and I've decided to go,' he said.

Stevie was very sad to see Michael leave but he knew how much he wanted to play abroad for a big club. 'We'll miss you, mate,' he said, giving Michael a hug. 'I understand – the chance to become a *galactico* is a dream come true. Good luck!'

Michael had been Liverpool's top goalscorer for years. Without him, what would they do? Rafa had a great idea.

'I want Didi and Xabi to play deeper in midfield,' he told Stevie when he called him into his office. 'I have a new role for you – I want you to get into the box and score goals!'

Stevie loved his new role behind the striker. He still did lots of tackling but it was really fun to push forward in attack. He had the energy to make great runs into the penalty area and his shooting got better and better.

'I've never scored more than ten goals in a season,' Stevie told Carra. 'This year, I'm going to beat that easily!'

In the final match of the Champions League group stage in December, Liverpool needed to beat Olympiacos by two goals to go through. Stevie loved playing against the best teams in Europe and he was desperate to stay in the tournament. The atmosphere at Anfield was unbelievable. The fans believed that their team could do it, and that inspired the players.

Olympiacos took the lead but Stevie didn't give up. 'We'll just have to score three!' he told his teammates at half-time.

Florent Sinama Pongolle scored the first Liverpool goal, and with ten minutes to go, Neil Mellor scored the second. 'We only need one more goal, lads. Come on, we can do this!' Stevie shouted. With the captain's armband around his sleeve, it was time to be a leader.

Liverpool played the ball down the left wing but Stevie was in lots of space on the right. 'Over here!' he called with his arms in the air. Eventually, Neil headed the ball back into Stevie's path. This was it – he needed to stay calm and get his technique right. Just outside the penalty area, Stevie struck the ball and it flew through the air and into the corner of the net.

Goooooooooooooooooooooooaaaaaaaaaaaaaaaaaaa alllllllllllllllllllllllllllllllllllllll!!!!!!!!!!

Stevie ran towards the fans, pumping his fists. It was a really special moment. At the final whistle, all of the players hugged each other. They still had a long way to go but Stevie was really pleased with the team spirit.

In the semi-final, Liverpool were up against Chelsea, the team that Stevie had nearly signed for. It would be a great feeling to beat them and reach the Champions League final. Ahead of the two games, Stevie and Carra swapped lots of banter with Frank and John about who would win. There was lots of pride at stake.

'We can't lose this, boys!' Stevie told his teammates in the dressing room. 'This is the biggest match of the season. We have to show that we're the best team in England.'

The first leg at Stamford Bridge finished 0–0. It was a good result to take back to Anfield but it wouldn't be easy. The Liverpool fans were louder than ever, singing the names of their star players.

Steve Gerrard, Gerrard
He'll pass the ball forty yards
He shoots the ball really hard
Steve Gerrard, Gerrard

After four minutes, Stevie flicked the ball through to Milan Baroš. The goalkeeper blocked Milan's shot but the ball bounced straight to Luis García. William Gallas blocked his shot but the ball was over the line. Goal! The Chelsea players complained to the referee but Liverpool had taken the lead.

'Stay focused!' Stevie shouted to his teammates as they celebrated.

The Liverpool fans cheered every pass and every tackle. Stevie never stopped running in midfield and Carra played the game of his life in defence. The second half seemed to go on for hours but at last, the referee blew the final whistle. Stevie and Carra hugged and danced around the pitch. Liverpool were in the Champions League final. All of the players partied late into the night.

'This is amazing!' Stevie said as he looked at all of the Liverpool fans at Istanbul airport. The whole city was painted red for the final. AC Milan were the favourites because they had great players like Andrea Pirlo, Kaká and Andriy Shevchenko but Stevie knew that they had a good chance of winning, especially with so much support in the stadium.

'I think the whole of Liverpool is here!' Carra joked as they travelled to the stadium for the game.

None of the players had slept because they were so nervous and excited. Playing in the Champions League final was the biggest match of their lives. In the dressing room, Stevie tried to inspire his team.

'We've done so well to get this far but if we win this, we will go home as heroes,' he shouted and his teammates cheered loudly.

When AC Milan scored in the first minute, the Liverpool players were shocked but Stevie told them to keep calm and carry on. By half-time it was 3–0 and most people thought the game was over, but not Stevie.

'Did you see the Milan players smiling and waving to their families?' he asked his teammates. 'They think they've already won this but they haven't!'

Manager Rafa's team talk was simple: 'Keep your heads up and remember that you play for Liverpool. Believe in yourselves and do it for the thousands of fans out there.'

The players sat and listened to the noise of the supporters. They never stopped singing. Stevie and the others were ready to fight in the second half.

A cross came in from the left and it was perfect for Stevie. He leapt into the air and used his neck muscles to power a header into the back of the net. As he ran back to the halfway line, he urged the fans to make even more noise. 'Come on!'

Two minutes later, Vladimír Šmicer scored Liverpool's second goal and suddenly, they were back in the game. They attacked the goal again and again.

'Be patient – we can do this!' Stevie shouted.

Didi played the ball forward to Milan Baroš,

who flicked it cleverly into the box. Stevie sprinted towards the ball but Gennaro Gattuso fouled him just as he was about to shoot. Penalty! Xabi's spot-kick was saved but he tapped in the rebound. It was 3–3! The score remained the same, even after thirty minutes of extra-time. The exciting final would have to be decided by penalties.

'Who wants to take one?' Rafa asked as the players rested on the grass.

'Me!' said Stevie, Vladimír, Luis, Djibril and John Arne Riise. Stevie would take their fifth penalty.

'Win this match for us!' they said to Jerzy Dudek as he went to take his place in goal.

Stevie stood with his teammates and cheered every goal. When Vladimír made it 3–2, the pressure was on Shevchenko to score. If he missed, Stevie wouldn't even need to take his penalty. Jerzy waved his arms and made the save. Liverpool were the winners! The whole team ran as fast as they could to celebrate with their goalkeeping hero.

Championes, Championes, Olé Olé Olé.

The players danced around the pitch and went

towards the fans in the crowd, who had been so important to the success of Liverpool.

'I told you we would win trophies!' Rafa said to Stevie and they laughed and hugged.

As captain, Stevie still had a big job to do. Lifting the trophy was the best feeling ever. Clouds of red smoke flew into the air and the players roared.

Liverpool, Champions of Europe. Stevie was on top of the world.

CHAPTER 17

THE GERRARD FINAL

'How many goals did you get last season?' Paul Jr asked his brother as the family relaxed at home in Huyton over the summer. Even when Stevie wasn't playing football, they usually still talked about it. After all, they were both Liverpool fans and they were looking forward to the next season.

'Thirteen in all competitions,' he replied. 'It's my best yet but I can do better.'

'Do you think you can score twenty?' Paul Jr asked. He knew how much his brother loved a challenge.

'Sure, why not?' Stevie laughed.

Stevie was a key goalscorer for the team now and

he enjoyed the responsibility. Whenever he could, he rushed forward to get in good positions for shooting. Liverpool were chasing Manchester United at the top of the Premiership but they truly excelled in cup competitions. They thrashed Birmingham 7–0 in the FA Cup quarter-final and then beat Chelsea 2–1 in the semi-final.

'Another trip to the Millennium Stadium!' Stevie joked with Carra as they celebrated the victory.

The final, held in Cardiff in May 2006, would be the last match of an excellent season for Stevie. Liverpool finished third behind Chelsea and Manchester United in the league, but he won the PFA Players' Player of the Year and there was still one last chance to win a trophy.

'There's no such thing as an easy final, boys,' he told them in the dressing room. 'And there's no such thing as favourites. If we don't play well, we will lose. Let's make this *our* FA Cup final!'

Their FA Cup Final opponents, West Ham, started really well and after half an hour they were leading 2–0.

'Come on boys!' Stevie shouted. 'We're half asleep – we need to get going in this game!'

Stevie got the ball deep in midfield and looked up. They needed him to do something special. Djibril was making a run behind the West Ham defence. It was the kind of long-range pass that Stevie loved to play. The ball landed right at Djibril's feet and he volleyed it powerfully into the net. Thanks to their captain, Liverpool were back in contention.

'This is like Istanbul all over again!' Djibril joked. 'Let's get another goal.'

West Ham defended well but Stevie knew he just needed to get into the right areas to score. When Peter Crouch headed the ball down to the edge of the penalty area, Stevie was there waiting. Instead of calmly placing the ball in the corner, he smashed it into the top corner.

'Game on!' Stevie shouted as he ran back for kick-off.

They were flying but out of the blue, West Ham took the lead again. Liverpool attacked relentlessly but they couldn't find another goal. On this hot

May afternoon, the players were tired and time was running out.

Rafa brought on Didi and shouted instructions to Stevie. 'Push forward!'

In injury time, the ball fell to Stevie. He was over thirty yards from goal and his legs felt heavy but he knew that it would take something spectacular to take the game into extra time. He was having a brilliant match – what did he have to lose?

As soon as the ball left his foot, Stevie knew he had hit it perfectly. He watched as it travelled like an arrow past all of the defenders and into the bottom corner.

Goooooooooooooooooooooaaaaaaaaaaaaaaaaaaaaaa allllllllllllllllllllllllllll!!!!!!!!!!!!!!!!

Stevie had saved the day yet again for his team. The adrenaline was rushing through his body. He had just become the first player ever to score in FA Cup, League Cup, UEFA Cup and Champions League finals. As he celebrated next to the fans, he pointed to the name on his back: 'GERRARD'. With every important goal, he became more of a Liverpool legend.

Both teams struggled through extra time. Penalties would decide the final again.

'I'm ready to take one!' Stevie told Rafa. As captain, he needed to lead by example.

Stevie sent Shaka Hislop the wrong way to make it 3–1. John Arne scored and when Pepe Reina saved Anton Ferdinand's penalty, the match was over. The whole team ran to celebrate with Pepe but Stevie was the real hero.

'They'll call that "The Gerrard Final",' Carra said as they jogged around the pitch, clapping and waving to the fans. Stevie loved the sound of that.

CHAPTER 18

WORLD CUP HEARTBREAK

It had been a long and exhausting club season but in the summer of 2006, Stevie and Carra were excited to represent their country in the biggest tournament in the world. For the World Cup, staged in Germany, most of the players from Euro 2004 were in the squad again and there were great expectations for England's 'golden generation'.

'Paraguay, Trinidad and Tobago, and then Sweden,' Stevie said, looking at the schedule. 'We can do this!'

England won their first two games and Stevie scored a great goal against Trinidad and Tobago with his left foot. Confidence was really high in the camp, especially with Wayne Rooney returning from injury. Manager Sven-Göran Eriksson rested Stevie for the final group match against Sweden but even then, he came off the bench and scored a header to force a draw. Stevie felt unstoppable.

In the second round, Beckham scored a free-kick to beat Ecuador and set up a re-match against Portugal. Stevie couldn't wait for revenge.

'We'll beat them this time!' he said and they all believed it.

It was a very tight match and the Portuguese defenders kept fouling Wayne. Everywhere he went, they pulled his shirt and kicked his ankles. Stevie could see that his teammate was getting frustrated.

'Stay calm and we'll score,' he told him. 'Don't let it get to you.'

The referee blew the whistle and Stevie thought it was just another free-kick to England. But the referee gave Wayne a red card! He couldn't believe it.

'Ref, what did he do?' Stevie asked.

'He stamped on the defender,' he replied.

Stevie knew Wayne well and there was no way

that he would have done that on purpose. It must have been an accident.

'Come on lads, we just have to keep going,' Stevie said, trying to lift his teammates' spirits. They were angry about the sending off but they were even more determined to win.

The match was still 0–0 after 120 minutes. It was time for penalties yet again and Stevie was ready to play his part.

'This time, we have to win this,' he told his teammates. They couldn't lose to Portugal on penalties twice.

Simão Sabrosa scored but Frank's shot was saved. Portugal had the advantage. Stevie stood on the halfway line with his teammates and waited for his turn.

It felt like such a long walk to the penalty spot but Stevie took deep breaths and tried to stay focused on scoring. He took penalties all the time and his country was relying on him. He was ready but the referee took ages to blow his whistle. Suddenly, Stevie started to doubt himself. There was so much pressure on him, both in the stadium and back home in England.

Stevie ran up and kicked it towards the bottom corner but he knew he hadn't got it right. The goalkeeper guessed where it would go and made the save. With his head down, Stevie walked slowly back to the halfway line. He couldn't look at his teammates; he had let them down badly. At Liverpool and in training, he scored every time. What had gone wrong?

England were knocked out and Stevie sat down in the centre-circle with tears in his eyes. It was the worst feeling in the world. He tried to think ahead to the prospect of winning more trophies but the defeat was really hard to accept. It had been one of England's best chances to win a World Cup since that summer of 1966, forty years earlier.

'It's time to move on, son,' Paul Sr said when Stevie returned to Liverpool. 'Remember, you'll have more chances to win that trophy.'

CHAPTER 19

DEADLY DUO PART I: STEVIE & FERNANDO

'Fernando Torres!' Stevie said excitedly. His brother had called him while he was relaxing by the pool on holiday. He had some big transfer news. 'Are you sure?'

'Yes, we've just signed him for £26.5 million,' Paul Jr replied. 'He's exactly the kind of world-class player that you need around you.'

'Finally, we've got someone else to score some goals!' Stevie joked.

He was really pleased to hear that the club would have a new superstar striker. It was a few years since the glory days when Robbie Fowler and Michael Owen would each score twenty goals a season.

Stevie had seen Fernando play lots of times for Atlético Madrid and Spain. He was one of the best young strikers in Europe.

'Welcome to Liverpool,' Stevie said to Fernando, shaking his hand as he arrived for pre-season training.

Fernando was quick, clever, and a brilliant finisher. The one doubt that people had about him was whether or not he was strong enough for the Premier League. The defending was much more physical than in La Liga, and he looked skinny. Stevie knew there was only one way to find out.

'When he first gets the ball, give him the biggest tackle you've got,' he whispered to Carra. Carra smiled; he loved a big tackle.

Fernando fell to the floor but he didn't complain. He got back to his feet and looked for the ball again. When Stevie passed it to him, he flicked it past Carra before he could even try to stop him. Fernando ran through and shot the ball into the bottom corner.

Carra looked at Stevie and nodded – Fernando was

definitely strong enough for the Premier League. He had the determination of a top striker.

'I've got a good feeling about this partnership,' Stevie said to Fernando as they walked off the training pitch. 'The Premier League better watch out!'

The more they played together, the better they understood each other. When Stevie got the ball in midfield, he always knew where Fernando was and where he would move next. Everything was so easy. They didn't need to talk about it; they could read each other's minds. With Fernando holding the ball up, Stevie was scoring more goals than ever.

In April 2008, against Blackburn Rovers, Stevie made his 300th appearance for Liverpool in the Premier League.

'Are you really only twenty-seven?' one of the younger players joked with him. 'You've been around for ages!'

'Don't be so cheeky,' he replied, giving a friendly slap. 'I'll be around for plenty more years, especially when our youngsters are so rubbish!'

During the Blackburn game, Stevie ran forward with the ball. There were lots of defenders around him but he could see Fernando in space. He passed and then kept moving towards goal. Fernando flicked the ball through for the one-two and Stevie placed the ball past the goalkeeper. 1–0!

In the second half, Stevie received the ball on the right wing. Without even thinking, he crossed it towards the back post. Fernando slipped away from his marker and headed the ball down into the bottom corner. 2–0! It was Fernando's thirtieth goal of the season and Stevie wasn't far behind him.

'You're unstoppable!' Rafa said at the final whistle, with one arm around each of his superstars. With Stevie and Fernando, they really could win the Premiership.

As they went into their final game of 2008 against Newcastle, Liverpool were top of the league and Stevie believed that they could go all the way. With Fernando injured, he needed to keep scoring. Stevie got the first and the fourth goals as Liverpool won 5–1.

'We just have to keep doing what we're doing,'

he told his teammates after the match. 'We're the best team in England right now but there's still half a season to go.'

Liverpool struggled in January and February and suddenly Manchester United were back at the top of the table. Stevie wasn't happy. He was so competitive and he hated to see the team throwing everything away.

'It's no good beating Chelsea but then losing to Middlesbrough,' he shouted angrily, throwing his shinpads to the dressing-room floor. 'We have to stay focused in every game!'

By March, Fernando was fully fit again, just in time for a massive month. First up, they played Real Madrid in the Champions League. Stevie loved playing against the top European clubs and he knew that they had a great chance of winning.

'If we get an early goal, they won't know what's hit them,' he told Carra as they got ready to run out at Anfield. They could hear the incredible noise of the crowd, like it was a twelfth player for Liverpool.

Fernando scored the early goal and Stevie made

it 2–0 from the penalty spot. At half-time, it was all looking good but Stevie refused to relax.

'We can't switch off, boys. We've got forty-five minutes to go!'

Two minutes into the second half, Ryan Babel crossed from the left and Stevie made his trademark run to the penalty spot. As the ball arrived, he smashed it into the top of net.

Goooooooooooooooooooooooooaaaaaaaaaaaaaaaaaalllll llllllllllllllllllllllllllllll!!!!!!!!!!!!!

The Kop went wild as Stevie ran past with his arms outstretched. The fans loved big European nights and this was one of the biggest.

The game finished 4–0 but after a short celebration, it was back to the Premier League and another very important match, against title rivals Manchester United.

'I don't think I've ever wanted to win a game more,' Stevie told his dad the night before. He was so excited that he couldn't sleep. 'If I don't score, I know Fernando will and vice versa. This is the best team I've played with. We have to win this!'

Even when United took the lead, Stevie didn't stop believing. Five minutes later, Fernando broke free and equalised.

'That's it – come on boys!' Stevie shouted, pumping his fists.

Just before half-time, Fernando spotted Stevie's run down the right. His pass was perfect but just as Stevie got to it, Patrice Evra fouled him. Penalty! Stevie placed it perfectly into the bottom corner. He was so happy to score that he kissed the Liverpool badge on his shirt and then the TV camera lens.

Liverpool defended really well and in the last fifteen minutes, they scored two more goals.

'4–1 – we destroyed them!' Stevie cheered at the final whistle, as he hugged Carra. He was so proud of his team's performance and now they were right back in the title race, four points behind with nine games to go.

Under Stevie's leadership, Liverpool kept winning. He even scored his first ever hat-trick against Aston Villa but unfortunately, Manchester United kept winning too. At the end of the season,

Liverpool were still four points behind. It was really disappointing to come so close to winning the league but they had given everything.

'Well done, lads,' Stevie said, patting everyone on the back. 'This time, we finished second. Next time, we'll finish first!'

CHAPTER 20

CAPTAIN OF ENGLAND

'His record is amazing – AC Milan, Real Madrid, Roma, Juventus.'

'I hear he has really strict rules. He looks scary!'

The England players were excited about their new manager, Fabio Capello. Some of them were worried that he would be too cold and tough but Stevie loved hard work and discipline. It's what the team needed in order to succeed in a major tournament.

'Stevie, you're one of my three key senior players,' Fabio told him at the first training camp. 'You, John Terry and Rio Ferdinand will be my captains on the pitch.'

Stevie was pleased to hear that. Capello's style

was very similar to Rafa's at Liverpool. He was very professional and focused on qualifying for the 2010 World Cup. To get there, John would be the official leader and Stevie would be his second-in-command.

In November 2007, a defeat to Croatia meant that England didn't make it to the European Championships in Austria and Switzerland. Within a year, after seven wins in a row, England faced Croatia again – this time in order to secure World Cup qualification – and they needed revenge.

'We're in great form, lads,' John told his teammates in the dressing room before kick-off. 'We've got nothing to fear. Let's go out there and show them how far we've come in the last year.'

England were so determined to win. In the first ten minutes, Frank scored a penalty and after that, they were unstoppable. Stevie spread the ball wide to Aaron Lennon and ran towards the back post. Aaron's cross was perfect and Stevie powered his header into the far corner of the net. He pumped his fists and high-fived his teammates.

'Come on, let's thrash them!' Stevie shouted.

In the second half, Frank scored again and then Wayne flicked a ball back towards the penalty spot. He knew that Stevie would be there and he headed the ball into the roof of the net. 4–0! Stevie slid towards the corner flag on his knees. In front of 80,000 England fans, they were playing some brilliant football. There was a party atmosphere at Wembley. Everyone was looking forward to the big tournament in South Africa.

Capello made Rio Ferdinand his new captain but just one week before the World Cup began, he picked up an injury at a training session. So the England manager called Stevie into his office.

'Congratulations, you'll be our captain for the tournament,' Capello said. 'I need you to lead by example, just like you do at Liverpool.'

Stevie nodded with a big smile on his face. Captaining his country at a World Cup was a dream come true. He would do everything to make his nation proud.

In the first match against the USA, Stevie made a

great run forward in attack. Emile Heskey saw it and cleverly flicked the ball through. In the penalty area, Stevie poked the ball past the goalkeeper with the outside of his right foot.

Goooooooooooooooooooaaaaaaaaaaaaaaaalllllllllllllllll lllllllllllllllll!!!!!!!!!!!!!!!!!!!!!!

England were off to a great start and the whole team celebrated together. They were in control of the game until Clint Dempsey took a long-range shot. There wasn't much power on it but as Rob Green went to catch the ball, it slipped through his fingers and into the goal. It was a bad mistake but Stevie needed his players to keep going.

'Forget about that, lads,' he shouted, clapping to encourage his teammates. 'We've got plenty of time to score another goal.'

England couldn't get a winner but a draw wasn't a bad first result. After a boring 0–0 draw against Algeria, England had to beat Slovenia to go through to the second round. Stevie was playing on the right of midfield, instead of his preferred role in the middle. It wasn't his favourite position but he would play anywhere to help his country. It was such a relief when Jermain Defoe scored the crucial goal.

'We need to do much better,' Stevie told his teammates, 'but at least we're through!'

Next up were England's biggest rivals, Germany. Stevie knew they would have to play the game of their lives to win. Germany took the lead after twenty minutes but England didn't give up. At 2–1, Frank hit a great shot that smacked the crossbar and bounced down over the goal line. The players started to celebrate but the linesman said that the ball hadn't crossed the line.

'That should have been a goal!' Stevie shouted to the referee. 'Even I could see that it went over the line.'

It was no use; in the end, Germany were just too skilful. They scored four goals, two of them by Thomas Müller, and England were knocked out of the World Cup. It was another disappointing tournament for their 'golden generation'.

'We did our best but it wasn't good enough,' Stevie said to Wayne as they slowly left the pitch in Bloemfontein.

STEVEN GERRARD

He loved being the England captain but time was really running out for Stevie to win an international trophy.

CHAPTER 21

GETTING OLDER

'You're getting older, son,' Paul Sr reminded Stevie as he rested his leg in front of the TV. 'You have to take more care of yourself now. You can't rush about the pitch flying into tackles all the time like you used to.'

Stevie had injured his Achilles tendon and he hated not playing football. Liverpool were struggling in mid-table and there was nothing that he could do to help. He was used to playing through pain but this time he had to take a break.

'If you keep playing, you'll do even more damage,' the Liverpool physio Chris Morgan warned him. 'You have to rest!'

Stevie didn't want his career to end at thirty and

so he did as he was told. With more than a month on the sidelines, it took him a while to get back to full fitness. After Xabi Alonso had gone to Real Madrid, Stevie was playing a deeper midfield role again. But just as he was finding his form once more, he suffered another injury – this time, much worse.

As he did a Cruyff Turn in a training match at Melwood, Stevie felt an intense pain in his upper leg. He had had groin problems for years but this felt serious. Stevie hobbled off the field and went straight to the physio.

'You've got two options,' Chris explained to him as he lay on the treatment table. 'Either you can have surgery now and be out for a few months, or you can see if it heals itself.'

'If we do nothing, there's a good chance that you could lose a lot of power when you kick the ball,' the surgeon told him.

Stevie thought about his favourite cross-field passes and his long-range shooting. There was no way that he could risk losing his power. 'Let's do the surgery,' he said.

'Good choice,' the surgeon said with a confident smile. 'Frank had the same operation and he was back playing again within three months.'

It was the end of Stevie's season but hopefully he'd be raring to go for pre-season in July. The surgery was successful and he had a great new scar to show off. But as Stevie began doing his strengthening exercises, he was still in a lot of pain.

'Okay, you need to rest for a bit longer,' Chris told him, as he checked the injury. 'Be patient – it still needs time to heal.'

Patience wasn't one of Stevie's strengths. When he went on holiday to Portugal with his wife Alex and the kids, he asked Chris to go too. In the afternoons, the family relaxed in the sun but in the mornings and evenings, Stevie worked hard in the gym.

'Do you think I'll be ready for July?' he asked. The exercises still hurt but it was getting better.

'Let's keep our fingers crossed and wait and see,' Chris replied. The worst thing they could do was to rush Stevie's recovery.

In the end it was September before Stevie could

play again. He was so happy as he came on as a substitute after six months out.

'I'm back!' Stevie said to himself. He had missed football so much.

By the time that Manchester United came to Anfield in October 2011, he was back to full fitness. As Stevie led his team out on to the pitch, there was a really serious look on his face. Liverpool needed a victory and he was determined to be the hero.

In the middle of the second half, they won a free-kick just outside the Manchester United penalty area. Charlie Adam picked up the ball to take it, and Stewart Downing was there too. They were both very good at free-kicks but Stevie didn't care.

'I've got this one,' he said. He was in the mood to score.

Stevie struck the ball low and hard into the bottom corner. The Manchester United goalkeeper didn't even move. Stevie felt so much joy that he thought his chest might explode. It felt so good to be back to his best for Liverpool. As the fans went wild in the Kop, Stevie ran straight towards them, pointing. He slid along the grass on his knees and kissed the club badge on his shirt.

After such an emotional game, the slight pain in his ankle didn't seem like anything to worry about. But as Stevie walked along the Anfield corridors, Chris saw him and he saw the swollen ankle. They rushed Stevie to hospital and caught the infection just in time. But Stevie didn't feel lucky; he just felt really low.

'Chris, I'm thirty-one years old and I think it's the end for me,' he said. He couldn't look his physio and friend in the eyes.

Chris took him to see Steve Peters, a renowned sports psychiatrist. Stevie was nervous as he arrived on crutches but they talked and talked about how he was feeling.

'What is your biggest worry?' Steve asked.

'Not being able to play football again,' Stevie said immediately.

'Are you happy at home?' Steve continued. He wasn't scared to ask personal questions.

'Yes, my family are amazing. I have a wonderful wife and three beautiful daughters.'

'Is that more important to you than football?'

Stevie nodded. 'Of course.'

'You need to stop worrying about your career,' Steve told him at the end of their first meeting. 'I've spoken to your doctors and they have no doubts that you'll be back. You have to focus your mind back on to your family and the trophies you've already won.'

It all made sense and with Steve's help, Stevie started to get back to his old, confident self. He had three or four years left as a footballer and, with a new hero in the Liverpool squad, Stevie was determined to make the most of that time.

CHAPTER 22

DEADLY DUO PART II: STEVIE & LUIS

'Welcome to Liverpool,' Stevie said to Luis Suárez as he arrived at Melwood for his first training session. Fernando had signed for Chelsea and the club needed a new star striker. Luis cost £23 million after scoring numerous goals in Holland. But how would the Uruguayan enjoy rainy mornings in England?

Carra was ready to test Luis just as he had tested Fernando back in 2007.

'The Dutch league is nothing compared to the Premier League,' Carra said. 'We need to see if he's ready to step up to the next level.'

Even at a five-a-side practice match Luis ran around like it was a cup final. He was everywhere, calling for the ball and then dribbling past defenders and scoring goals. When the other team had the ball, he never stopped fighting and chasing. He didn't give the defenders a single second to think. Liverpool definitely had a new superstar.

'He's the most annoying striker I've ever played against,' Carra complained as they left the field. He was exhausted and embarrassed. 'I think he's even better than Fernando!'

Stevie couldn't wait to see Luis play in a proper match. He liked being one of the best players at Liverpool but world-class teammates always brought the best out of him. To match Luis's talents, Stevie worked harder than ever. He wasn't as quick as he used to be but he still had the experience and vision to play great passes, especially when he had strikers ahead of him making such clever runs.

In the League Cup Final in February 2012, Liverpool were up against Cardiff City – a particularly big game for Stevie and his family.

'Looking forward to Wembley?' Stevie texted his cousin, Anthony. After starting at Everton, Anthony

Gerrard was now Cardiff's centre-back. They couldn't wait to play against each other.

'Of course! The underdogs are ready for a shock win,' Anthony texted back.

'I have family pride resting on this game,' Stevie told his teammates in the dressing room before kick-off. 'If we go into this match thinking it'll be easy, they'll beat us. Let's give it everything and win another trophy!'

Cardiff scored first but in the second half Luis headed the ball towards goal and it hit the post. The ball bounced to Martin Škrtel and he scored the rebound. In extra time, Liverpool had lots of chances to score and finally, Dirk Kuyt put the ball in the net. Stevie thought they'd won it but Cardiff equalised right at the end. It was time for another penalty shoot-out.

With his teammates standing together on the halfway line, Stevie made the long walk to take the first penalty. He placed the ball on the spot and as he walked back for his run-up, he focused on where he would place his shot. He aimed for the top left corner but it didn't quite go high enough and the goalkeeper made a great save to tip it onto the crossbar and over. Stevie slowly moved back to his teammates with his hands on his head. They patted him on the back and told him not to worry, but Stevie hated to let his team down.

Charlie hit Liverpool's second penalty over the bar and suddenly they were in real trouble. Luckily, Dirk, Stewart Downing and Glen Johnson all scored and it came down to Cardiff's fifth taker – Stevie's cousin Anthony. Anthony hit a low shot but it went wide of the post. Liverpool were the winners.

Stevie felt really sorry for Anthony but his teammates were piling on top of their goalkeeper, Pepe Reina, and he ran to join in. After more than a year of injury problems, it was a great feeling to walk up the steps and have a winner's medal placed around his neck. As Stevie raised the trophy into the air, the Liverpool fans cheered wildly.

'Congratulations on your first English trophy!' Stevie said to Luis. 'Are you happy?'

Luis smiled. 'I'm very happy but this is just the start. I want to win many more.'

Stevie loved Luis's ambition; it was exactly what

Liverpool needed to become a better team. Like Stevie, Luis hated losing more than anything in the world. Together, they were forming a great partnership in attack. Luis was a great goalscorer but he was also very good at creating goals for others.

In the Merseyside derby against Everton, the ball came to Stevie on the edge of the area. The goalkeeper was off his line and so Stevie calmly lifted the ball into the back of the net with his left foot.

Goooooooooooooooooooaaaaaaaaaaaaaaaaaaaaaaaall!!!

Early in the second half, Luis cut inside from the right wing. He nutmegged one defender and then dribbled past a second. He was nearly in a position to shoot but he saw Stevie running forward. As he arrived, Luis stepped back and Stevie smashed the ball into the net.

Stevie ran to the fans, holding up two fingers for two goals. Then he looked around for Luis and when he came running over, he gave him a big hug.

'Thanks, what a run!' Stevie shouted over the noise of the celebrating Liverpool fans.

A hat-trick against their local rivals would be one of the best moments of Stevie's career, and he was desperate to score one more goal. In injury time, an Everton midfielder slipped and Stevie dribbled forward. Luis ran to the left and Stevie passed to him. Two defenders closed Luis down and so he cut inside and passed back to Stevie, who was now in lots of space. Stevie put the ball in the net and pointed to Luis with a huge smile on his face.

'You're the best!' Stevie said as they hugged again.

In his first full Premier League season for Liverpool, Luis scored twenty-three goals. Every time he got the ball in attack, he looked dangerous. Defenders backed away, or tried to foul him, but Luis was unstoppable. All he needed was more support and Liverpool made two more formidable attacking signings: Daniel Sturridge from Chelsea and Philippe Coutinho from Inter Milan.

As Stevie watched the skill and speed of Luis, Daniel and Philippe, he got really excited. 'Next season, I really believe that we can win the league!'

CHAPTER 23

THE SLIP

'They're calling us "SAS"!' Daniel Sturridge said after another great victory. In a 4–1 win over West Brom, Luis Suárez had scored three and Daniel had scored one. There was a fun rivalry between the two of them about who could score the most goals.

'There should be a third "S" in that!' Raheem Sterling added. The young winger's pace and trickery was causing lots of problems for Premier League defences.

'And a "C"!' Philippe Coutinho added.

'And a "G"!' Stevie Gerrard said and everyone nodded. Their captain was their leader. In his deeper midfield role, he was the one that started every move with his brilliant passing. Stevie's experience was so important with lots of young players in the side.

On Christmas Day 2013, Liverpool were top of the Premier League but after defeats to Manchester City and Chelsea the following week, they slipped down to fifth.

'We're playing so well against the lower teams,' Stevie said to his teammates at the start of 2014, 'but we have to do better in the big games.'

The first big test of the new year was Arsenal. The Liverpool manager at the time, Brendan Rodgers, told his players to start strongly. 'I want us to attack as much as possible in the first fifteen minutes. If we run at the Arsenal defence with our pace and movement, they won't be able to handle it. And once we get one goal, we'll get many!'

They certainly listened to their manager's instructions. In the first minute, Stevie curled a great free-kick into the box and Martin tapped it in.

'That's it!' Stevie shouted as they celebrated. 'Let's keep going – they'll be nervous now, so let's score a few more.'

Stevie was the creator again, as Martin scored a brilliant header from his corner kick. Then Luis played the ball across the penalty area and Raheem made it 3–0. Liverpool were just too good for Arsenal and the match finished 5–1.

'What a performance!' Stevie said at the final whistle as he went round high-fiving all of his teammates. 'Thirteen more games like that and we'll be Premier League champions!'

After three wins in a row, Liverpool were now back at second place in the Premiership. When they went to Old Trafford, the squad were full of confidence, and Stevie had no doubt that they could win. In the crowd, the Liverpool fans showed off a huge new banner that said 'MAKE US DREAM'.

After fifteen minutes, Daniel crossed to Luis at the back post. As he controlled the ball and tried to play it past the defender, it struck his arm. Handball! Penalty! Stevie had missed a few important penalties during his career but he never stopped believing that he could score. He placed the ball carefully on the spot and then waited with his hands on his hips. When the referee blew the whistle, Stevie sent the goalkeeper the wrong way and put his shot right in the corner of the net.

'That's a perfect penalty!' Raheem said to Stevie, giving him a big hug.

He loved scoring against Manchester United and the fans knew how much it meant to him.

Steve Gerrard, Gerrard
He'll pass the ball forty yards
He shoots the ball really hard
Steve Gerrard, Gerrard

At the start of the second half, Liverpool won another penalty. As Stevie stepped up to take it, the fans wondered where he would put his second spot-kick of the match – in the same corner as the last one, or in the opposite corner? Stevie knew exactly what he was doing and even though the goalkeeper went the right way this time, his shot was right in the corner.

Stevie ran and did his trademark knee-slide along the grass. He was so happy to play a big part in Liverpool's best title challenge in years. The whole team huddled together to show just how strong they were. In the last few minutes, Luis made it 3–0.

'We can do this!' Stevie shouted in the dressing room after the game and his teammates cheered loudly.

Four more wins later, Liverpool were top of the league with five games to go. They were close but they still had two massive matches left – Manchester City and then Chelsea.

It was an emotional day as Stevie led his team out on to the pitch for the first of these matches. It was now twenty-five years since the Hillsborough disaster. Stevie touched the 'This is Anfield' sign and thought of his cousin Jon-Paul. He would be so proud of how well Liverpool were doing. As the minute's silence ended, 40,000 Liverpool supporters roared around the stadium – it was game time.

'Come on, we're ready for this!' Stevie screamed to his teammates.

Raheem made a great run from the left to the right. Luis's pass was perfect and he controlled the ball, tricked a defender and then put the ball in the net. It was a dream start and the whole team piled on top of Raheem. Then from a Stevie corner, Martin Škrtel scored another header. He slid on his knees towards Stevie and they hugged and rolled around the grass. They felt unstoppable.

But in the second half, Manchester City scored two quick goals and suddenly the pressure was on Liverpool to find a winner. Stevie's head went down for a second but he quickly got back to urging his team to attack.

'Keep going, get forward!' he yelled.

City had lots of chances to score again but Liverpool refused to give up. Players like Stevie and Luis had brought a winning mentality to the team. A clearance fell to Philippe Coutinho on the edge of the penalty area and he curled the ball first time into the bottom corner.

Goooooooooooooooooooooaaaaaaaaaaaaaaaaaaaaaa llllllllllllllllllllllllllllllllll!!!!!!!!

At the final whistle, Stevie gathered his players together in a huddle. 'This isn't over yet,' he told them. 'This does not slip now! This does not slip!'

The players cheered and turned to clap the fans, who were singing 'We're going to win the league'. Liverpool were still on track to win the title for the first time in twenty-four years. First, however, they had to beat Norwich, Chelsea, Crystal Palace and Newcastle.

The Chelsea match was the biggest match of Stevie's career. After fifteen years in the Liverpool first team, he had an amazing opportunity to win the Premiership, the best league in the world.

Chelsea's manager José Mourinho knew all about Liverpool's quick starts and so he slowed the game down as much as possible. Liverpool didn't have many chances and they grew more and more frustrated.

In the last minute of the first half, Stevie came deeper into defence to get the ball. Demba Ba, the Chelsea striker, rushed to close him down. The ball slipped under Stevie's foot and as he ran to get it back, he fell to the floor. He was in trouble. Ba ran through and scored past the goalkeeper. It was a big mistake but the Liverpool fans were supportive.

Stevie Gerrard is our captain
Stevie Gerrard is a red
Stevie Gerrard plays for Liverpool
A Scouser born and bred

In the dressing room, Liverpool manager Brendan Rodgers tried to lift the spirits of his players. 'We need to stay calm. It's only 1–0 and we have plenty of time. You're trying too hard.'

Stevie was desperate to make up for his error in the second half but the Chelsea defence was too good. It was the worst moment of his career as Stevie walked off down the tunnel. Liverpool had lost and it was his fault.

'Remember all of the amazing things that you've done for the club,' Rodgers said as tears streamed down Stevie's face. 'Remember all of the trophies that you've won, and remember that incredible night in Istanbul. You're a Liverpool legend and they'll never forget that.'

Against Crystal Palace, Liverpool were 3–0 up. Stevie was feeling a bit better after helping to set up two of the goals.

'Come on, we can still beat Manchester City to the title!' Stevie shouted as they celebrated.

But in the last ten minutes, it all went wrong. Crystal Palace scored one, then another and then another. It was 3–3 and they couldn't believe what had happened. At the final whistle, Luis lifted his shirt over his face and cried and cried. They had all worked so hard and they had got so close to winning the league. It was a terrible feeling. Stevie helped Luis to his feet. He pushed the TV cameras away and walked with his teammate off the pitch.

'We did our best,' Stevie said. 'We should all be very proud.'

CHAPTER 24

THE END

'I feel so old!' Stevie said as he lay down on the treatment table while Chris massaged his back. He howled in pain; his whole body ached. It was getting harder and harder to play ninety minutes of fast Premier League football.

'Well it's a good thing that you're off for a holiday in the USA then,' Chris replied with a cheeky smile on his face. He would miss his favourite Liverpool player.

After months of thought, Stevie had decided to follow David Beckham and Frank Lampard by concluding his career as a player in the American MLS (Major League Soccer). It was the most difficult decision he had ever made and as his big farewell got nearer and nearer, he wondered if he was making a mistake.

'Are you sure you want to go? LA is very different to Liverpool!' his brother Paul Jr kept asking.

'Don't leave – we still need you!' his teammates told him.

But as he limped from the physio room to his car, Stevie knew that it was time to move on. He had played seventeen amazing seasons in the Liverpool shirt but he was ready to let the club's new generation of footballers take over.

Stevie's last game at Anfield was an unforgettable day. As he walked out on to the pitch with his daughters, the fans held up cards that spelt out 'SG8' and 'CAPTAIN'. Stevie tried really hard not to cry as he listened to a stadium full of fans singing his name. They had shared so many incredible victories together – the Champions League Final in Istanbul, the FA Cup Final in Cardiff – and he would miss them so much. It was really hard to leave his beloved club.

'Skipper, we've got something for you,' Jordan Henderson said, holding out a book as the team ate dinner together.

The players had collected nice messages from lots of Stevie's teammates, managers and opponents: Robbie Fowler, Fernando Torres, Luis Suárez, Kenny Dalglish, Brendan Rodgers, even Zinedine Zidane.

'Wow!' Stevie couldn't believe it – it was the best gift that he had ever received.

As he read through the pages, his head was full of happy memories. There had been so many highs and lows over the years, but Stevie had loved every minute of his career for Liverpool and England. What an adventure it had been. Through hard work and the support of family, friends and coaches, the skinny local lad had become a Liverpool captain and legend.

STEVEN GERRARD HONOURS

Liverpool
★ FA Cup: 2000–01, 2005–06
★ League Cup: 2000–01, 2002–03, 2011–12
★ UEFA Cup: 2000-01
★ UEFA Super Cup: 2001 UEFA Champions League: 2004–05

Individual
★ PFA Young Player of the Year: 2001
★ PFA Team of the Season: 2001, 2004, 2005, 2006, 2007, 2008, 2009, 2014
★ Ballon d'Or Bronze Award: 2005
★ UEFA Club Footballer of the Year: 2005

STEVEN GERRARD

★ UEFA Team of the Year: 2005, 2006, 2007
★ PFA Players' Player of the Year: 2006
★ England Player of the Year: 2007, 2012
★ FWA Footballer of the Year: 2009

Turn the page for a sneak preview of
another brilliant football story by
Matt and Tom Oldfield. . .

LUIS SUÁREZ
EL PISTOLERO

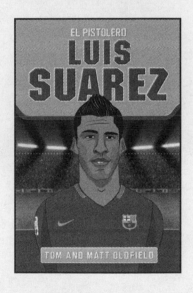

Available now!

978 1 78606 012 9

CHAPTER 1

CHAMPION OF EUROPE

6 June 2015. As Luis took a quick glance around the stadium, all he saw were the colours of Barcelona. It was still thirty minutes before kick-off but they were cheering as if the warm-up was the real thing. He stretched out his right leg, loosening the muscles and preparing his body for the biggest game of his life.

Xavi fired the ball towards him, catching him by surprise, and Luis turned to chase it as it rolled off the pitch. As he crossed the touchline, almost within touching distance of the Barcelona fans in the front row, all he heard was 'Suárez! Suárez!' He grinned and gave the fans a quick wave. They were ready for this Champions League Final – and so was he.

Hard times make you appreciate the good times – that had been Luis's motto over the past year. After all the anger, the tears, the headlines and the four-month suspension, he had bounced back better than ever. There was nothing he could do about his mistakes in the past, except try to learn from them. He had shut out all the distractions and focused on only two things: football and family. Now, having already won the Spanish league title and the Spanish Cup, he was ninety minutes away from completing an amazing Treble.

Back in the dressing room, Dani Alves turned the music up loud and the players tried their best to relax. Luis walked over to the far side, where the 'Suárez 9' shirt was hanging. He had worn that name and number plenty of times but it had never looked better than it did now. He looked up at the countdown timer high on the wall – less than fifteen minutes to go. He put on the shirt, pulled up his socks and slotted in a tiny pair of shin pads. Their opponents, Juventus, would play a physical style, but

Luis had never liked big, bulky shin pads. He could handle the kicks.

'Dani, throw me the tape,' he called.

'Do I work for you now?' Dani replied, laughing. 'Just because you score the goals, you think you run the place?'

Luis had quickly built good friendships within the Barcelona squad. For the first time since leaving Uruguay, he was surrounded by teammates who spoke Spanish, and that had certainly helped him to settle in quickly. He still had to pinch himself to believe that he was scoring goals alongside a magician like Lionel Messi.

The referee knocked on the dressing-room door. It was time. Luis finished putting the tape round his wrist, jumped to his feet and joined in the quick high fives. As they headed for the tunnel, he felt a hand on his shoulder and turned to see Xavi waiting with some final words of advice. 'Stay calm out there. They know all about your temper and they'll be trying to wind you up. Play your game and ignore them. We need you.'

Luis nodded. Many of the things he regretted most in his football career were related to reckless moments on the pitch. He just needed to win every game, and sometimes he went too far. 'Don't worry. I won't let you guys down,' he added with a serious face. Then a grin broke out. 'After the game, it'll just be my goals that people are talking about.'

For most of his teammates, this was yet another Champions League Final. But it was Luis's first and he was shaking with a combination of nerves and excitement. The atmosphere was incredible – the anthem, the fans, the perfect pitch. It was like no other game he had ever played.

As he passed the ball around in a little triangle with Messi and Neymar, he had no doubts about the result of the game. With all their star players, how could they not score three or four goals? He placed the ball in the centre circle. He would be getting the first touch of the final! When the whistle blew for kick-off, Luis felt like he could run all day.

Barcelona took an early lead and Juventus equalised in the second half, but Luis struggled to find his best form. Was it just the big occasion that was getting to him? He worked hard but nothing was falling for him. With twenty-five minutes to go, he even feared that he might be substituted. Clapping his hands, he urged his teammates to do more, saying, 'Leo, let's go. Let's make something happen.'

One of Luis's biggest strengths was that he never gave up and always believed that a chance would come his way. From his earliest years, he just knew where to be at the right moment to score goals. There's still time, he told himself. Things can change in a second.

Then it happened. Messi dribbled past three Juventus defenders, and Luis saw his teammate preparing to take a shot. His instincts took over. He wasn't going to watch the shot. As soon as Messi pulled his leg back to shoot, Luis was racing towards the goal, looking for a rebound. Juventus goalkeeper Gianluigi Buffon made the save but the ball bounced loose. None of the defenders had a chance. Luis was too quick. Before they could move, he had pounced on the ball and fired a shot into the top corner.

Suddenly, as the emotions took over, everything was a blur. He jumped over the advertising boards onto the athletics track that surrounded the pitch. Lionel, Neymar, Dani and the rest of his teammates joined him, climbing on his back and burying him in hugs. He had saved the day. 'That was such a classic Suárez goal,' Dani yelled. 'You shoot, you score – that's why you're El Pistolero!'

As he jogged back to the halfway line, Luis couldn't stop smiling. He loved scoring in big finals. From the first time he kicked a ball, he had always wanted to be the goalscorer and the hero. While the game was stopped for a substitution, he allowed his mind to wander, just for a minute, back to his beloved Uruguay, where it all began.

COLLECT THEM ALL

SERGIO AGÜERO
THE LITTLE GENIUS

ZLATAN IBRAHIMOVIĆ
RED DEVIL

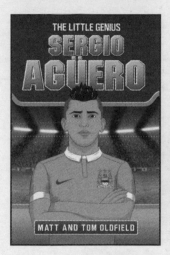

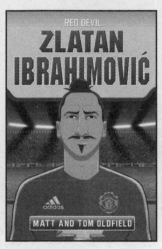

The Little Genius is the tale of the boy who would go on to re-write football history forever. His dramatic 94th minute goal on the final day of the 2012/13 season, to snatch the title from under rivals Manchester United's noses, was the most electric moment in Premier League history. This is how the small boy from Argentina became the biggest hero of all.

978 1 78606 218 5
£5.99

Zlatan Ibrahimović: Red Devil follows the Swedish superstar on his amazing journey from the tough streets of Malmö to becoming the deadly striker at Manchester United. Along the way he has been a star for Juventus, Inter Milan, Barcelona, and Paris Saint-Germain, as well as becoming Sweden's all-time leading goal scorer. This is the story of one of a generation's finest footballers.

978 1 78606 217 8
£5.99

COLLECT THEM ALL

ALEXIS SÁNCHEZ
THE WONDER BOY

LUIS SUÁREZ
EL PISTOLERO

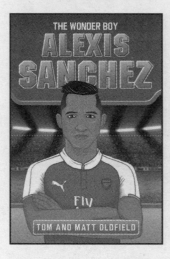

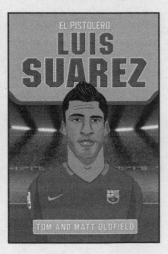

Alexis Sánchez: The Wonder Boy tells the story of the Arsenal superstar's incredible journey from the streets of Tocopilla to become 'The Boy Wonder', a national hero, and one of the most talented players in the world. With his pace, skill and eye for a goal, Alexis is now one of the Premier League's biggest stars. The story is every bit as exciting as the player.

978 1 78606 013 6
£5.99

Luis Suárez: El Pistolero follows the Uruguayan's winding path from love-struck youngster to Liverpool hero to Barcelona star. Grabbing goals and headlines along the way, Luis chased his dreams and became a Champions League winner. This is the inspiring story of how the world's deadliest striker made his mark.

978 1 786060129
£5.99

COLLECT THEM ALL

EDEN HAZARD
THE BOY IN BLUE

GARETH BALE
THE BOY WHO BECAME
A GALÁCTICO

Eden Hazard: The Boy in Blue is the thrilling tale of how the wing wizard went from local wonder kid to league champion. With the support of his football-obsessed family, Eden worked hard to develop his amazing dribbling skills and earn his dream transfer to Chelsea.

978 1 78606 014 3
£5.99

Gareth Bale: The Boy Who Became a Galáctico tracks the Welsh wizard's impressive rise from talented schoolboy to Real Madrid star. This is the inspiring story of how Bale beat the odds and became the most expensive player in football history.

978 1 78418 645 7
£5.99

COLLECT THEM ALL

WAYNE ROONEY CAPTAIN OF ENGLAND

RAHEEM STERLING YOUNG LION

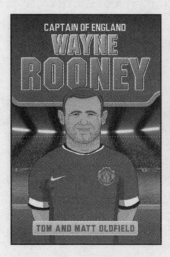

Wayne Rooney: Captain of England tells the action-packed story of one boy's journey from the streets of Croxteth to one of the biggest stages in world football. This heartwarming book tracks Rooney's fairytale rise from child superstar to Everton hero to Manchester United legend.

Raheem Sterling: Young Lion is the exciting tale of a boy who followed his passion and became one of the most dynamic young players in world football, winning the hearts of Liverpool and England fans along the way. Relive Sterling's whirlwind journey in this uplifting story.

978 1 78418 647 0
£5.99

978 1 78418 646 3
£5.99